the
TEEN
QUIZ
BOOK

the
TEEN
QUIZ
BOOK

by
Annalee Levine, Jana Johnson,
and Arlene Hamilton Stewart

Andrews McMeel
Publishing

Kansas City

www.andrewsmcmeel.com

98 99 00 01 02 SOL 10 9 8 7 6 5 4 3 2 1

Library of Congress Cataloging-in-Publication Data

Levine, Annalee.
    The teen quiz book / by Annalee Levine, Jana Johnson, and Arlene Hamilton Stewart.
        p.   cm.
    ISBN 0-8362-5415-5 (ppb.)
    1. Teenage girls—United States—Life skills guides. 2. Teenage girls—United States—Conduct of life. 3. Questions and answers—United States.   I. Johnson, Jana.   II. Stewart, Arlene. III. Title
HQ798.L48   1998
305.235—dc21   97–47056
                                                                              CIP

Book design and composition by Lisa Martin

ATTENTION: SCHOOLS AND BUSINESSES

Andrews McMeel books are available at quantity discounts with bulk purchase for educational, business, or sales promotional use. For information, please write to: Special Sales Department, Andrews McMeel Publishing, 4520 Main Street, Kansas City, Missouri 64111.

Contents

Chapter Three.
Feeling Super:
The 411 on Health
and Exercise

Chapter Four.
Acting Cool:
How You Handle Yourself

Chapter Five.
Teachers and Attitudes:
What's Happening in School

Chapter Six.
Home Life:
Parents, Sibs, and Your Space

Chapter Seven.
Hot Looks:
Fashion and Beauty

INTRODUCTION

If you're like us, you love reading teen magazines. Most likely, the first thing you search for are the quizzes. Why? Because they're all about us. And unlike math or bio quizzes, they're totally fun to take!

In fact, we think they're so much fun we've put together a whole book of nothing else, dozens and dozens of quizzes about romance and love, your friends, family, fashion—all the good stuff. You'll discover how cool you are when you "Rate Your Come-ons" and check out your love skills in "Guy Talk: Is He Reeling You In or Speaking His True Mind?" And speaking of truth, we dare you to find out how much you know about health and fitness in "How Buff Are You?" or challenge your own attitudes in "Are You *Too* Into Your Looks?"

Along the way, we hope you make some discoveries about yourself like we did. We're both in high school, and believe us, we've been there—dating disasters, fashion bummers, bud troubles, divorced families. Guess you could say we're pretty average teens! But on the plus side, we have learned lots from our experiences and have tried to cram the goods in here for you. So pick up a pen, rock back, and have a great time learning more about a really cool teen—you!

CHAPTER ONE

THE GUY FILES
Crushes, Steadies, and Exes

From the second you first lock on to his extra-long eyelashes to the moment you tear up his yearbook photo in a jealous rage, you'll find a teen's love life is loaded with more major ups and downs than your dad's blood pressure. How do you handle it? How do you figure out why crushes act the way they do? How do you know if love will last? And most of all, how do you avoid mistakes?

To keep your love life babelicious, check out our crush-worthy quizzes. Be totally honest with yourself, because when it comes to The Guys . . . the more you know, the more you score.

do **his** moves
mean "i like you"?

All guys have opening moves that smart girls pick up on. It's their way of letting you know that they like you without having to say or do anything risky. Knowing how to read their signals gives you an advantage because it allows you to act with confidence. Answer yes or no if your hottie is doing any of these.

1. He invites you on a study date to help prepare for the big exam.
Y___ N___

2. He says hi to you in the hall. Y___ N___

3. He sits behind you in math class. Y___ N___

4. He asks you to go on a double date with his brother and your best friend. Y___ N___

5. He shows up at a few of your soccer games.
Y___ N___

6. He drops you a birthday card with a simple "Happy Birthday" inside.
Y___ N___

7. When you see him at a party he comes over and asks you to dance.
Y___ N___

8. When he finds out that you got a new car, he asks for a ride home.
Y___ N___

9. He calls to find out the homework.
Y___ N___

10. He asks you for advice on what gift to get for his sister.
Y___ N___

11. He "happens" to bump into you a lot.
Y___ N___

12. When he promises you something (to lend you his calculator, a new CD, etc.), he delivers.
Y___ N___

13. He knows your middle name.
Y___ N___

14. He buys you a soda, without you even asking.
Y___ N___

15. He's starting to look better and better.
Y___ N___

Your Score

6 or more "Yes" answers: He's Into You. Stay with it. This guy is showing you the right signals. Give it time; there's potential to go farther.

3 to 5 "Yes" answers: Could Be, Stay Cool. Stick with it. He might be just getting to know you. Something could develop.

2 or more "Yes" answers: Borderline Boy. Wait it out a little bit, but if more signals don't appear, move on fast! You could be wasting your time.

Is He Boyfriend Material?

Sure, your crush is a heartthrob, but is he right for you? Discover if he's into you or not worth dreaming about.

1. **You spot your crush after school sitting with his friends. He acknowledges you by:**
   A putting his head down and continuing to talk to his friends.
   B saying hi and coming over to talk.
   C making eye contact but not saying hi.

2. **You answer the phone around dinnertime and it's him. He's calling to:**
   A ask if your best friend still likes him.
   B make plans for the weekend.
   C ask about the math homework.

3. **You see him at a soccer game on Saturday afternoon. He talks to you about:**
   A every girl as she walks by, speaking highly of each one's nice features.
   B the new movie in town, and he invites you to go with him.
   C your own sports game.

4. When he discovers that you won class president, he reacts by:

A saying he'll see you for dinner, but never showing up.

B giving you a congratulatory hug and asking you out.

C giving you a high five.

5. When you find out that you have a major final project due, he:

A asks if he can copy your paper to get an easy A.

B asks to be your partner and does half the work.

C says that he works best on his own.

6. For your birthday he:

A what birthday? He didn't do anything.

B secretly organizes a great surprise birthday party.

C sends you a birthday card in the mail.

7. On an average day you see him:

A once, when he asks for a ride home.

B three or four times.

C twice: at lunch and after school when he is hanging out with his buds.

8. When a friend asks you to pose together for a picture for the yearbook he:

A says, "No thanks."

B puts his arm around you and holds you tight.

C stands close to you and gives a grin to the camera.

9. **When he finds out that you got detention he:**

   A flips out. How is he supposed to get home now? Take the bus?

   B waits for you after school and brings you your favorite flavor milk shake to cheer you up.

   C says he's sorry, and he'll catch you later.

10. **You need help studying for a test. When you ask him he says:**

    A "Sorry, I need to study alone. Maybe next time."

    B "I'll be over in five minutes."

    C "Maybe we can get together during lunch for some last-minute cramming."

Your Score

Mostly As: No Way! You would get more respect and compassion from your big brother. Try to find a guy that will give you more attention and treat you properly. Also be aware that he may be using you, especially if Daddy just bought you that new car.

Mostly Bs: The Perfect Fit. This guy is hot after you. He knows how to treat you and appreciates everything you do. He likes to have free time with his buds, but loves spending quality time with you. The organizing of a surprise party was a clue of his true feelings toward you.

Mostly Cs: Just a Friend. Although this guy may like you, he may enjoy just being your friend. His friendly affection toward you is good, but friendly may be as far as it is going to go.

Am I good at getting
him to notice me?

You've always had a crush on this hunk. At last it is time to make your move. Before doing anything drastic, take this quiz to find out if your moves will take you straight to Love Land or Single City. First, check true for the moves you would make and false for the ones that you wouldn't consider. Then check the end to see how you scored. You get one point for every correct choice.

1. The day you met your crush, you introduced yourself as "Jane, your stalker."
❏ **TRUE** ❏ **FALSE**

2. In chemistry class you volunteer to be hunky's lab partner.
❏ **TRUE** ❏ **FALSE**

3. At lunch, you spot him from across the cafeteria and decide to walk by and say hello.
❏ **TRUE** ❏ **FALSE**

4. At a party on Saturday night, you ask him to dance.
❏ **TRUE** ❏ **FALSE**

5. When your hunk moves in next door, you bake a batch of welcome-to-the-neighborhood cookies and hand-deliver them.
❏ **TRUE** ❏ **FALSE**

6. The second you discovered that his favorite color was black, you bolted to the mall and bought a new black wardrobe.
❏ **TRUE** ❏ **FALSE**

7. If you're lucky enough to catch his eye, you swear that you'll bare a little more skin each day, hoping he'll talk to you.
❑ TRUE ❑ FALSE

8. The day his girlfriend dumped him, you called to express your sympathy, then asked him out on a date.
❑ TRUE ❑ FALSE

9. Although you have never spoken to him, just gazed at him, you drop several secret-admirer notes by his locker.
❑ TRUE ❑ FALSE

10. When he fails the math test that you just aced, you volunteer to tutor him.
❑ TRUE ❑ FALSE

11. You wear soft, sexy clothes that totally warm his heart.
❑ TRUE ❑ FALSE

Answers

1. **False**. Although it's good to introduce yourself with your name, think about leaving out the stalker part. It'll scare him away.

2. **True.** Volunteering to be his lab partner is a great idea. Also, it will give you a great excuse to call him once in a while for the homework or to study for a test together.

3. **True**. Saying hi is a good way to get his attention. Just be careful not to spill your milk or trip on a chair.

4. **True**. Asking him to dance could get you close, especially if you are dancing to a slow song. If he declines your offer, forget about this guy and consider someone else.

5. **True**. It will soften not only his heart but his family's too. Just be sure you sample a cookie before making the trip to his house.

6. **False**. Save your gas. Wearing his favorite color to school every day will not capture his heart. It'll just make you look silly.

7. **False**. Baring more skin may get his eye, but it'll reel him in for the wrong reason. Stick to showing off your mind, not your body.

8. **False**. They just broke up, so lay off and give him time to breathe. He most likely isn't in great spirits, so let him be. It'll turn out better in the long run.

9. **False**. A note or two might be nice, but if you do it too often, you'll only spook him. Also, sooner or later he'll find out who the sender was, and you may end up feeling and looking childish.

10. **True**. Tutor him . . . but for real. Better grades will also get you in good with the family. Remember, helping him doesn't mean giving him the answers, just helping.

11. **True**. Dressing hot will warm not only his heart but other body parts as well. Don't go too far.

Your Score

7 to 11 points: Boy-Stalker Plus. You really have the game of love down, and with your artistry you should have no trouble bagging the guy of your dreams.

4 to 6 points: Would-be Heartbreaker. The time to study up on moves and gamesmanship is now. Remember, if you don't think a move is cool, it's probably not.

0 to 3 points: Things Can Only Improve! Love is a game that is never boring, never over. There are no real losers when you learn from the past. Stay in there, keep your eyes open, and you'll get on great.

Love Signals:
Ten Shoo-ins That He Has
Fallen HARD for You

You're in love big-time. Are your feelings being returned? Answer yes or no to learn if your crush is as into you as you are into him.

1. He's your number one fan at all of your sports games, even away ones.

❑ **YES**
❑ **NO**

2. He makes you a photo album of all the fun times you've shared.

❑ **YES**
❑ **NO**

3. He shows up at your door with a dozen roses ... just because.

❑ **YES**
❑ **NO**

4. He creates a collage of all your inside jokes and gives it to you.

❑ **YES**
❑ **NO**

5. He calls every night just because he misses you.

❑ **YES**
❑ **NO**

6. He invites you to his brother's wedding.

❑ **YES**
❑ **NO**

7. He walks you home after school holding your hand.

❑ **YES**
❑ **NO**

8. He calls your parents and organizes a surprise birthday party for you.

❑ **YES**
❑ **NO**

9. He plans a picnic at your favorite outdoor place.

❑ **YES**
❑ **NO**

10. He writes a love poem and slides it into your locker.

❑ **YES**
❑ **NO**

Your Score

7 or more yes answers: Head Over Heels! Hang on to this boy. He is truly in love with you, and it shows.

5 or more yes answers: In Love! This guy has fallen hard for you. Make sure you let him know that you feel the same way.

2 to 5 yes answers: In Lust. This guy is into you, but he may not be in love. Keep him; he has great romantic potential.

0 to 2 yes answers: Not Good Enough. Better keep your options open and look for a more caring crush.

Rate Your Come-ons: The **BEST** and **WORST** Things to Do

Hi, is anyone sitting here?" Corny come-on? Maybe, but sometimes a girl has to take the sitch in her own hands to break the ice with a shy guy. Fortunately, flirting can be learned without painful trial and error. Rate your flirting power to see how you measure up. Circle the come-ons closest to your personal scoping style.

Move 1 (worth 10 points)
There he is, hot babe at twelve o'clock. Your buds have scoped him out, too. You decide to:

A. join the stampede.
B. cruise offshore until the coast is clear.

Move 2 (worth 10 points)
You're next to this love hunk, but he seems like a mute. To get him to talk to you, you:

A. break the ice by smiling and softly saying hi.
B. ask him his name and where he's from.

Move 3 (worth 5 points)

The distance to first base is sixty feet. It might as well be sixty miles. You're getting nowhere flirting with this guy. You:

A. increase your drooling.
B. move on to another player.

Move 4 (worth 10 points)

You walk into a hot party filled with new guys. What's your tactic?

A. Check out the whole scene first before making your move.
B. Zoom in on the first dream dude you see.

Move 5 (worth 5 points)

Which is cooler to do?

A. Clutch a hottie's arm to punctuate a story.
B. Lightly brush his sleeve when walking away.

Move 6 (worth 15 points)

You like this guy and sense something is coming back, but you've been standing in the same place for half an hour. You should:

A. make up some good reason to move on, leaving him with a smile.
B. stick to him until the party ends.

Move 7 (worth 15 points)

You walk into study hall. It's totally empty except for Brainiac Babe! Wow! How do you get to sit next to him without looking like a transparent dork?

A. Walk past his seat, then drop all your books next to him.

B. Ask him if he has seen your pen (or book or whatever), which you're sure you left right where he is sitting.

Move 8 (worth 10 points)

Mega-Hunk walks into the cafeteria where you're hanging with your male buds. To get his attention, you:

A. start to laugh hysterically at everything the guys say.

B. lock into eye contact and send him a soft smile. Your tractor beam will pull him in.

Move 9 (worth 10 points)

You suddenly find yourself sitting next to Hunky-Monkey at a basketball game. You:

A. concentrate on the game, cheering when your team makes great plays and casually make eye contact.

B. yell loudly, stand and stomp at every opportunity, and grab his arm "accidentally" during an exciting play.

Move 10 (worth 10 points)

This is the third time you've run into him in the school hall. Now he stops to chat, but after that—nothing! How do you get this guy to move off his space and ask you out?

- A. Say, "I've got two tickets to the Rolling Stones. Would you like to go?"
- B. Hang in there, give him a grin, but don't cling. Casually compliment him on something he did. If he still doesn't bite, move on fast.

Scoring

1. B. Never compete in a group. Flirting is a solo act. You're smart to wait until he's alone.

2. A. Always keep part of yourself back, but appear friendly. Being overeager is a major turnoff.

3. B. Move on! If you hang in too long, you look desperate. There are plenty of great guys for a cool girl like you.

4. A. Always survey the field before making a move. Parties are shopping trips, too.

5. B. In the beginning, never be pushy. Too much touching can be misread as being too easy.

6. A. Don't overexpose yourself. Guys need to be made to want to chase you.

7. **B.** Good opening. Then casually slide your books down next to his. Apologize for disturbing him, which requires an answer on his part, then chat for a minute or two. If he seems interested, sit down. If not, move on!

8. **B.** Coming on with buds just to get somebody else's attention is obvious and stale. Plus, your buds will think you're an idiot!

9. **A.** Sure you're tense and can hardly watch the game, but you've got to at least look interested in something he digs.

10. **B.** You've got to stay in control. If he thinks you're sweet and approachable, he'll open up. Don't scare him off with an offer that's inappropriate.

Your Score

75 plus: Top Speed. You're cruising fast and your moves are classy as a Mercedes. You handle yourself well.

50 plus: Range Rover! You're polishing up your act. Flirting takes practice, so stay in the game; you're getting better.

25 plus: Pull Over. We have to talk. Think about this: Guys like girls who don't appear pushy. Yes, there is a difference between assertive and aggressive. It's called success.

25 and below: Learner's Permit. So you don't know all the moves now—you'll learn. Always remember with guys, less is more. The right move is the light move.

Sure **Cures** for the Uncommon **Crush**

Listen up. Sooner or later everybody gets totaled by a mega-crush. You know, the kind of crush where you can't eat, can't sleep, can't stop obsessing about him. Where you know his wardrobe—and his schedule—better than your own! If this is where your crush-crazy head is at, take our Sure Cure Crush Control quiz . . . and give yourself (and everybody else) a break.

1. Your friends invite you out for pizza, but you've been praying hard all week he'll call. Should you:

☐ take your cell phone with you and think about him every moment you're out?

☐ bail on your buds to gaze at his photo in the yearbook all night?

☐ leave an elaborate message on your answering machine in case he calls?

If you checked any of these, you qualify for the Sure Cure: Go with the buds and have fun—but hang the cell phone up at home. If he calls and it's important to him, he'll call back. Besides, any chick is way more attractive if she's not so easily available.

17

2. You can't close your locker/crush shrine because it's overstuffed with crush memorabilia. Should you:

☐ go to the school office and request an additional locker?

☐ beg your friends for a little of their space?

☐ start carrying your gym clothes to class?

Check any of these answers? You need a Sure Cure: Clean it out! You're making a spectacle of yourself. Bag that stuff and make some room for your own life.

3. Your binder and textbooks are tattooed with his initials. Now you're eyeing your bedroom wall. Should you invest in:

☐ a new set of binders and erasable pens?

☐ a gallon of whiteout?

Sure Cure: Stop putting his bogus stamp all over everything; it's overkill and not cool. Besides, he won't feel flattered. Clean up your act with new covers and keep your feelings a little more under wraps. Soon you'll feel better.

4. **On your fifth lap around his house, you begin to feel like a stalker. Should you:**

☐ cut your routine down to two loops a day?

☐ buy a new pair of sneakers so you can pretend to be trying out for the track team?

Sure Cure: So what if you steal a glance at him? Go for the new shoes, but head for the track for real. Work out and get your head into a healthy new groove. After a few sessions, you'll feel better about yourself and stop obsessing about him.

5. **The phone bill has skyrocketed since the crush kicked in. Instead of calling him endlessly and hanging up when you hear his voice, you should:**

☐ pretend to be in telephone sales.

☐ have your buds call for you.

Sure Cure: Actually talk to him. Ask him what the math assignment is or whatever. A dose of reality will make you see him more as a person, not just a love object.

6. **Every day you check out his horoscope in the newspaper, but lately you've begun to notice that it's not giving you any hard information. Do you:**

☐ get his time of birth, go to an astrologer, and have an expensive year-long chart done up?

☐ switch to numerology instead?

Sure Cure: Ditch both of these ideas fast. Horoscopes are fun, but they're no real substitute for observation and judgment. Gaze a little more at your own life rather than dreaming about his.

7. **You notice he likes to grab an early-morning cup of joe in the school cafeteria and you want to appear cool, too. After downing three cups hoping he'll show up, you're overwired. Should you:**

☐ switch to decaffeinated?

☐ drink more slowly?

☐ order a muffin?

Sure Cure: Spend that time going around the track, rather than tracking him down. You'll feel and look healthier, plus you could meet some yummy runners in the process.

8. **His favorite color is blue, so now every-thing you wear is blue, too. Your buds think you're whacked and tell you:**

☐ to cool it and be yourself.

☐ you look bad in blue.

☐ that's what his old girlfriend wore.

Sure Cure: Cool it and be yourself! You want him to like you for yourself, not because he feels he's looking in the mirror. Wear your favorite color and let him come after you.

Crossovers:
When Does a Bud Become a BOYFRIEND?

He's been your bud forever. In fact you feel like he's your brother. Suddenly one day there's a new vibe in the air. Could it be that Cupid's arrow has scored a direct hit? Cruise through this quiz to see if you're crossing over into Romance Land, or if it's just the stars playing with your heart.

Check true or false after each question:

1. When you leave him after a study session, funny things he said float into your mind.
T___ F___

2. When it's time to leave a party, you find yourself checking out who's with him.
T___ F___

3. When he tells you about his new crush, you feel bothered.
T___ F___

4. He's starting to put his arm around you more often. T___ F___

5. You used to run into him a million times a day and never notice. Now you find yourself looking for him. T___ F___

6. When you look up in math class, you catch him gazing at you.
T___ F___

7. His friends start to ask if you would ever like him. T___ F___

8. It's midnight on a rainy Saturday night, and you long to talk to him.
T___ F___

9. For the first time, you wonder how you should sign his birthday card. "Love"? "Your Pal"? "Hugs and Kisses"?
T___ F___

10. You've always borrowed his things, even his clothes. Now you don't want to return his sweater. T___ F___

11. You hope that you look good when you walk past him. T___ F___

12. Once you went to dances as buds. Now you're uptight about the homecoming dance.
T___ F___

13. You find yourself packing the supermarket cart with all his favorite stuff. T___ F___

14. You notice he's finding lots of reasons to talk to you. T___ F___

15. When you used to watch tapes together and romantic scenes came on, you'd goof on the actors. Now you're tense.
T___ F___

16. You worry about whether his feelings for you also have changed, and if he's ever going to make a move.
T___ F___

17. You're racking your brain to remember his favorite perfume.
T___ F___

18. When he bumped up against you in the cafeteria, you knew that it was him without even looking.
T___ F___

19. You find yourself wondering what he's doing when you're not there. T___ F___

20. Every time the phone rings, you wonder if it's him. T___ F___

Your Score

Mostly falses:

Relax, your love text is negative. It's probably just stress from schoolwork that's making your radar system go haywire. Take a weekend off to rest up and keep your bud in perspective.

Mostly trues:

The bells are ringing big-time, girl! These smoldering embers are about to burst into love flames. You can go from bud to beau, but keep it light in case you want to go back to being just friends. Otherwise you'll probably have a great romance with a great guy, because he's also a great friend.

What's LOVE Got to Do with It?

You think you could be ready for the big "S" word, but you're still having second thoughts. Before you take that big step, take this test to find out more about your true thoughts on sex.

1. **In your opinion, the most appropriate age to have sex is:**

   A whenever you feel that it's time. After all, if you like this guy it's okay.

   B after marriage.

   C when you really love someone and have hung out together for a little while.

2. **For protection you plan on using or already use:**

   A a condom, if he remembers.

   B abstinence—until marriage, that is.

   C the pill and a condom. I wouldn't jump if I didn't have a parachute.

3. **You wouldn't mind losing your virginity in this setting:**

   A a passionate moment in the back of his truck or car.

   B on your romantic honeymoon.

   C after a candlelit dinner in bed with the one you love.

4. You want to have a baby:

   A when you get pregnant; you love kids.

   B after marriage.

   C when you both have a good education and stable jobs.

5. You estimate that by the time that you turn eighteen you will have had ____ (how many) sexual partners.

   A where's that calculator?

   B none.

   C one, maybe two, if that.

6. In your opinion, how long should you generally date before becoming sexually active:

   A do you have to be "together" with him?

   B long enough to fall in love and get married.

   C when we're both in love and committed to each other.

7. Your ideal session of lovemaking would last:

   A an intense ten minutes.

   B an entire honeymoon.

   C until you both got tired.

8. You learned about sex from:

   A older siblings; they told you how to do it.

   B parents and church.

   C media, family, peers.

9. **Pop Quiz! The only form of birth control to prevent against pregnancy and sexually transmitted diseases (STDs) is:**

    A is there one that does both?

    B abstinence.

    C condom.

10. **When you finally decide to take that big sex step, it's because:**

    A your crush said it was time.

    B you're safely married.

    C you're truly ready. You trust and love him and you've considered the consequences.

Your Score

Mostly As: Slow Down, Tiger. Although you may think it's time, you have to decide for yourself if you really are ready for that huge step. Just because your crush said that it was okay doesn't mean that it is. In addition, be safe. Always use a condom. If he forgets, tell him to forget the sex part and just enjoy your company.

Mostly Bs: Conservative Lady. You respect the commitment that sex implies. You want to wait until you are married, and that may save you a lot of heartache. You'll probably be happy you waited.

Mostly Cs: On Target, Girl. You are worth waiting for and you know to always use birth control. In addition to using a condom, to be extra safe, use a backup like the pill.

NOTE: Although abstinence is the only 100 percent sure way to be safe from unwanted pregnancy and STDs, condoms are the only form of birth control that will provide fairly reliable protection against both.

Can YOU Read a **Hookup?**

Sure, last night was great, but was making out the beginning of a beautiful relationship or just an awkward situation? Hookups are incredibly hard to read, but with these helpful hints, you might find reading them easier. Check off how you feel about each situation.

1. After your "seven minutes in heaven," he asked your name (for the third time that evening).
❑ GOOD THING ❑ BUMMER

2. The next day, you got a call and a date for the weekend.
❑ GOOD THING ❑ BUMMER

3. When you spot him in the hall the day after, he puts his head down and walks right by.
❑ GOOD THING ❑ BUMMER

4. When your ecstasy was over, he left the party to go to his girlfriend's house.
❑ GOOD THING ❑ BUMMER

5. Your best friend calls to let you know that the rumor mill was churning all night. Apparently, your kiss has turned into losing your virginity.
❑ GOOD THING ❑ BUMMER

Your Score

1. "Good thing"? It is nice that he wants to know your name, but if he asks for it three times, he is defeating the purpose. **"Bummer"?** If he doesn't know your name, that's bad!

2. If you answered **"Good thing,"** bonus points for you! Give yourself a pat on the back—you just succeeded in a healthy hookup. This guy just may be for real. If not, don't worry, it may have been too good to be true.

3. "Bummer." What a coward! He needed to at least acknowledge you. However, if he did say hi, including your name, good job.

4. "Bummer." If he ditched you, think bad things. Especially if he was headed back to his girlfriend's house. Did you know he had a girlfriend? If so, shame on you.

5. You don't want someone that is going to kiss and tell. If you answered **"Bummer,"** forget about him, he wasn't worth your effort.

GUY TALK:

Is he **reeling you in** or speaking **HIS TRUE** mind?

Every girl's second language should be Guy Talk. Why? Because guys rarely come out and say what's really happening. To avoid hurting someone else's feelings or having a messy confrontation on their hands, they say other things instead. By doing your bilingual best to keep control of communication, you can minimize the potential for "misunderstanding." Check out how fluent you are at translating what Guy Talk means by matching "What He Says" to "What He Means."

What He Says:

1. ____ "I need some space."
2. ____ "You got a haircut?"
3. ____ "I'll call you."
4. ____ "Let's try just being friends for a while."
5. ____ "Susie sure looks hot today."
6. ____ "Help me study for math."
7. ____ "Why don't you ask Melissa over?"
8. ____ "I tried calling all weekend, but your line was busy."
9. ____ "You know you're the only one for me."
10. ____ "I'm not sure, but I think I have to help my grandmother on Saturday night."
11. ____ "You're a wonderful person."

12. ___ "Let's not do Valentine's Day. I'm broke.
    But I love you."
13. ___ "No, you don't look fat in that dress."
14. ___ "Where are your parents?"
15. ___ "I only kiss girls I'm crazy about."

What He Means:

a. Ouch! This dude's looking elsewhere now.

b. He had better things to do and forgot about you.

c. It's over.

d. Hey, porky.

e. Sucker!

f. He's been thinking hard about other chicks.

g. You're not the one for him.

h. It's the beginning of the end.

i. He may . . . or he may not.

j. Your hair totally sucks.

k. Beware, he may only want to study.

l. He doesn't want to spend the dinero on you.

m. Warning, he'll be out of your life soon.

n. Where's the bedroom?

o. As if!

Scoring

1. h	4. c	7. f	10. o	13. d
2. j	5. a	8. b	11. g	14. n
3. i	6. k	9. m	12. l	15. e

1 to 5 correct answers: **Red Alert! Translation Malfunction.** With your language skills, you shouldn't go out on the street, let alone after a guy. For a complete analysis of the play-by-play, try reading the dudes' body language more and observing their actions. Don't go by just what they say.

6 to 10 correct answers: **Vouz Parlez Bien.** But keep up those sensors, girlfriend, 'cause as good as you are, you still need some help. Especially with those action verbs such as *dump, dupe,* and *dis.*

11 to 15 correct answers: **Voice Control.** A mega-great listener and translator like you could work at the United Nations. You'll be running circles 'round the dudes and having mucho fun 24/7 !

CUTE CATCHES:
KEEP Them *or*
Throw Them **Back?**

You're reeling in the babe of the year... and are so blissed out! When your feet return to earth, you may want to consider whether your big-time Baldwin has more going on than just a gorge bod and dreamy eyes. Nobody is saying you can't hit a genetics jackpot and have brains, beauty, character, and sensitivity all wrapped up in one beautiful package—we just want you to read the labels carefully. Check the column that describes your catch: "Keeper" if he's like that or "Throw Back" if he's not.

	Keeper	Throw Back
I like that his exes are still his friends.		
His buds are so loyal.		
He'll do anything to help someone else.		
He's into working out and eating right.		
He loves his ratty old baseball cap.		
When he promises to pick me up, he's there.		

	Keeper	Throw Back
His abs are so buff.		
He looks like a *GQ* stud, but doesn't know it.		
He tells me I'm beautiful.		
We baby-sit together when I can't get out of it.		
I can tell him my deepest secrets and he keeps them!		
He makes me laugh.		
He face lights up when he introduces me.		
He never brags about helping others.		
He remembered *my* mom's birthday.		
He knows what college he wants already.		
I've never heard him whine.		
He loves to cook for me.		
He sends me sweet notes and drawings.		
Even though he doesn't necessarily get them, he tries out for lots of things.		

	Keeper	Throw Back
He never just blows off chicks who come on to him.		
With his huge grin, he always tries to cheer me up.		
He does lots of community service, and not just for the credit.		
I talk to him so much, I feel like his best bud.		
He never kisses up to the teach just to keep up his average.		

Your Score

If you answered mostly Keeper: All-around amazing! Smart, sexy, and fun! A dreamboat who's tied up at the dock for you.

Mostly Throw Back or below the halfway line: Always be on the jerk-alert for guys who are too into themselves. They have little endurance in two-way relationships.

Is It Okay to Go After a Guy?
How to Get a **Yes**

Who says only guys get to do the choosing and chasing? If your love life is hovering around zero, is it okay to take control? Some guys think it's cool when chicks make the first move, but others think it's way aggressive. How do you land a crush who's stuck in a shy groove without getting stung in the process? Check out these come-ons to see if your style is muy cool.

1. You've been having a ball with this brainiac babe in study hall for weeks. It's time to move into a higher gear. You want to say, "My parents are going away this weekend. Want to come over?"

Cool ___
Uncool ___

2. You finally asked him out and now you've got cold feet. Can you dump him?

Cool ___
Uncool ___

3. You're thinking of breaking up with your boyfriend 'cause you like his mega-babe bud better. Can you see if he's interested in you before the break?

Cool ___
Uncool ___

4. You're tired of waiting for him to come around, so the next time you see him you tell him exactly how you feel and ask him what his feelings are.

Cool ___
Uncool ___

5. Your crush's sister tells you he likes you. But when you call, he's never home. Do you decide to keep trying for another month?

Cool ___
Uncool ___

6. You want a guy who's modern in his thinking and not uptight about who makes the first move. When you learn your new crush is like that, you dig him even more and ask him out right away.

Cool ___
Uncool ___

7. You think he's shy, but so are you. You ask your bud to throw a party and invite his whole gang to take the pressure off.

Cool ___
Uncool ___

8. For years, you've dug this heart-stopping hunk. Now you're at the school dance and he looks *soooo* good. You ask him to dance and tell him he's the hottest guy in the whole place.

Cool ___
Uncool ___

9. Sometimes you call just to hear his voice, then hang up. Once you got busted on caller ID, but that didn't stop you.

Cool ___
Uncool ___

10. Last Saturday night you went out with him and it was so hot! Or so you thought. You haven't seen him at school and he hasn't returned your calls. You decide to slip a love note in his locker.

Cool ___
Uncool ___

11. You went out twice, but he didn't put any moves on you. You refer to him as your "boy-friend" anyway and resolve to ask him out the next time you see him.

Cool ___
Uncool ___

12. You've told all your buds about your crush. They go with you to buy him a Valentine's Day card that you send "anonymously."

Cool ___
Uncool ___

13. You know he loves art, so you ask him to help you out on the school float.

Cool ___
Uncool ___

14. You like him and sense it's mutual. He's into hoops big-time, so when your dad has two extra tickets to a Knicks game, you think of asking him.

Cool ___
Uncool ___

15. You're leaving school together and having a great time talking about music. You say, "Want to come over and hear the new Oasis album?"

Cool ___
Uncool ___

Scoring

1. **Uncool.** You'll give him the wrong idea.
2. **Uncool.** He has feelings, too.
3. **Uncool.** Don't try to cover all your bases at once.
4. **Uncool.** You haven't even gone out yet!
5. **Uncool.** The sis might be up to no good. Hang it up now!
6. **Cool.** You've found out what he's like.
7. **Cool.** A great, low-risk way to get together.
8. **Uncool.** You're really putting him on the spot.
9. **Uncool.** That's totally kid stuff!
10. **Uncool.** Unless he went to Disney World, he's ducking you!
11. **Uncool.** You look like an amateur at the game of love.
12. **Uncool.** Be out in the open or not at all.
13. **Cool.** A casual come-on is always best.
14. **Cool.** He can enjoy the game and your company.
15. **Cool.** Sharing common interests is a great lead-in to romance.

does he like me for me?
How to Tell if He's Worthy

Lately, have you been wondering if your guy likes you for yourself or for all the goodies that go with you? If you've been feeling shaky with your steady, maybe the time has come to ask yourself some tough questions. To avoid getting hurt—or to confirm he's the cool dude you thought he was—check in the column that applies to your sitch.

	No Way!	It's Happened	That's Him
He uses my e-mail as his own address.		—	—
He frequently borrows my car.	—	—	—
Asking for rides is this dude's specialty.	—	—	—
He suggests I print two copies of all my essays.	—	—	—
He goes home when his favorite foods run out.	—	—	—
My headset seems to be his.	—	—	—
Even on his half birthday he expects presents.	—	—	—
When it comes time to pay, he's always broke.	—	—	—
He encourages me to get a job.	—	—	—

	No Way!	It's Happened	That's Him
He plans his social schedule, then tells me.	___	___	___
I have to wear hot clothes to show off for his friends.	___	___	___
He was more excited about Mom's new car than I was.	___	___	___
Half the family's videotape collection is at his house.	___	___	___
He borrows my brother's clothes.	___	___	___
I always give him "bigger" presents than he gives me.	___	___	___
He's dropping hints about going on a family vacation—with us!	___	___	___
He thinks our pool is cool and invites all his friends over.	___	___	___
My cell phone has become his message center.	___	___	___
My locker is crammed with his junk.	___	___	___
He borrows money, but never pays it back.	___	___	___
He doesn't replace things he breaks.	___	___	___
If he does me a favor, he always reminds me.	___	___	___
He asks me to pick up food on my way to meet him.	___	___	___

Your Score

Mostly "No Ways!" **One Cool Dude.**

A guy this great is into you for real. Be good to
him, girl.

A few "It's Happened" **Dude Improvements.**

Not perfect, but if it doesn't happen too often, you
might consider keeping him to see if he shapes up
into the great guy you deserve.

A lot of "It's Happened" **User Unfriendly.**

He's in love with a wonderful guy: himself! You might
want to look at the fine print on this romance and
find yourself a more responsible guy.

Mostly "That's Him" **Bad to the Bone.**

Bail out big-time! This is a cad in the making. And
don't worry about breaking his heart—it was
never yours.

FALLING out of Love?
Danger Signals

Lately Mr. Right has seemed like Mr. Impossible. He's turned from charming to annoying and you are a tad worried. Is your relationship going downhill? Read this to find out if Mr. Right is really for you. Circle the answer closest to your heart.

1. Lately you've noticed his eyes wandering:

    A into your eyes.

    B toward other girls.

    C into space.

2. Your first month you spent every weekend together; now you spend:

    A every night together.

    B every other weekend.

    C time together during school. You're both so busy that you don't have any other time.

3. His nickname for you is:

    A he never calls you by name.

    B Princess.

    C just your name, nothing special.

4. For Valentine's Day he:

A made you a frame with a picture of you two together.

B got you carnations from the supermarket.

C forgot about it but promised to make up for it.

5. He knows how psyched you are for the prom. He shows up in:

A a hot tux.

B a nice jacket and a tie.

C jeans and a T-shirt.

6. The big English term paper is due next week and he hasn't started.

A He asks to copy yours.

B He says he'll see you in a week; he needs time to work on it.

C He invites you over so you can work and still be together.

7. It's Monday night and you two are supposed to study for math. But when he finds out that the big game is on, he:

A hangs with you and checks the game during study breaks.

B ditches you and says that he'll cram with you during lunch tomorrow.

C catches the first half with you, then goes to his friend's house.

8. You just failed your chem test and you're bummed. To cheer you up, he:

A comes over and offers to tutor you.

B says he's sorry and he'll call you later.

C teases you about it.

9. You went out of your way to make a special dish for a romantic dinner. He:

A tells you he loves it (even if you thought it was a little dry).

B tells you how it really tasted.

C refuses to finish and looks in the freezer for pizza.

10. Your cousins are in town and you're stuck with them for two weeks. He:

A heads for his friend's house.

B asks if they're babes.

C suggest that you all go to the amusement park.

Your Score

1. **A**-1, **B**-3, **C**-2	6. **A**-3, **B**-2, **C**-1
2. **A**-1, **B**-2, **C**-3	7. **A**-1, **B**-3, **C**-2
3. **A**-3, **B**-1, **C**-2	8. **A**-1, **B**-2, **C**-3
4. **A**-1, **B**-2, **C**-3	9. **A**-1, **B**-2, **C**-3
5. **A**-1, **B**-2, **C**-3	10. **A**-2, **B**-3, **C**-1

10 to 14 points: He's a Keeper. This guy is really into you. Hold on to him—great guys like this don't come around often.

15 to 20 points: Love Waiting. This guy likes you, but face it—he's not passionate, at least with you. He treats you decently but look for someone else for magic.

21 plus points: Drop Him. This guy is a real jerk. Stop wasting your time with him and find a guy who will respect you. You are his equal, not his slave, and you should be treated a lot better.

does **BREAKING UP** mean you **can't** Still **"BE FRIENDS"?**

You're broken up and totally bummed—worried that a guy you like as a friend won't want to be one. Take this quiz to find out whether he could turn into a great bud or if he just wants to be left alone. Check the answer most like you.

Before you fell head over heels, you were:
❑ a) friends forever.
❑ b) friends of friends.
❑ c) unaware of each other.

He thinks your friends are:
❑ a) cool girls. He doesn't mind splitting your time with them.
❑ b) total losers. He has a pet peeve about each one of them.
❑ c) okay chicks. He'd rather hang with you alone, but once in a while he doesn't mind hanging with them.

When you broke it off, you felt like it was _____ in the room.
❑ a) ice cold. You were rightfully bitter because he dropped you for a bozo.
❑ b) warm. You were bummed, but you left on fairly neutral terms.
❑ c) burning hot. His lame excuse left you steaming. This wasn't how you thought it was going to be.

Your relationship lasted:
- ❑ a) one month. You both decided that you were better off being friends.
- ❑ b) three months. You both changed and decided to see other people.
- ❑ c) nine months. The relationship ran its distance.

While you were together, he showed his affection by:
- ❑ a) locking lips between every class.
- ❑ b) holding hands while walking you to your class.
- ❑ c) Saying hi to you in the halls. Bonus points if he said hi in front of his pals.

For the anniversary of your first month he:
- ❑ a) brought you flowers. You dried them and hung them up.
- ❑ b) ooops! He forgot.
- ❑ c) made you a card with a simple "Happy Anniversary from Joe" on the inside.

Since you broke up two weeks ago, you've spoken to him:
- ❑ a) once. He called to see how you are doing.
- ❑ b) three times. It's hard not talking to someone that you miss.
- ❑ c) every night. He can't decide if he really meant to break up with you.

His other friends:
- ❑ a) still say hi, but you know that it is just to be nice.
- ❑ b) have spread rumors about the breakup to cover up for their friend and to make you look bad.
- ❑ c) treat you the same. Just because you and your ex aren't together doesn't mean that you can't be their friends.

Your 'rents are:

❑ a) glad to see him go. They never liked him anyway.

❑ b) sad. He was so good to you.

❑ c) okay with it. As long as you are happy.

Your shrine of him in your locker has recently:

❑ a) been torn down, but not until you took a black marker and drew devil's horns on his image.

❑ b) hasn't moved. You can't stand to take it down.

❑ c) been dismantled, except for your favorite picture of you two together.

Scoring

1. **A**-2, **B**-3, **C**-1

2. **A**-3, **B**-1, **C**-2

3. **A**-1, **B**-3, **C**-2

4. **A**-3, **B**-2, **C**-1

5. **A**-1, **B**-3, **C**-2

6. **A**-2, **B**-1, **C**-3

7. **A**-2, **B**-3, **C**-1

8. **A**-2, **B**-1, **C**-3

9. **A**-1, **B**-2, **C**-3

10. **A**-1, **B**-2, **C**-3

Your Score

10 to 15 points: Stay Away. Although this guy seemed great, your breakup has most likely left you a little bitter and put out. He wasn't the best boyfriend, and the way his friends are treating you lets you know what he is saying about you. Leave him and move on to someone better. He isn't worth the effort.

16 to 22 points: Possible Pal. This might work. Even though you may be upset about the breakup, give it a little time. He may be upset, too, and that will take time to heal, but you can still be friends. In the beginning, it might be difficult, but try it.

23 to 30 points: Stick with Him. This guy obviously wants to be your pal. He was a good boyfriend and deserves a second chance at friendship. You may find it awkward hanging out at first, but you do care about each other. Tell each other that you'll speak at least once a week, and promise to still hang out if possible.

dumper vs. dumpee:
which is BETTER or WORSE?

Just as it takes to hook up, it takes two to break up—the dumper and dumpee. Ouch! No matter what role you play, for sure they'll be some intense feelings. What do you think? Is it better to dump—or to be dumped? Fill out this checklist to discover if there is a better or worse side to "ENDING IT."

1. You wanted to end your romance but stuck with it. Now your crush is dumping you! Is it:

❏ **Better**
❏ **Worse**

2. Your boyfriend dumped you. What if your friends do, too? How would you feel about telling them your concerns?

❏ **Better**
❏ **Worse**

3. The relationship doesn't feel right. You decide to dump him before Valentine's Day. Do you feel:

❏ **Better**
❏ **Worse**

4. You've been dumped before and hate the way it feels. Now you end everything prematurely. Does that make you feel:

❏ **Better**
❏ **Worse**

5. You've always been the dumpee. Now your best bud, who's bragged that she's never been axed, just got dumped. Do you feel:

❏ **Better**
❏ **Worse**

6. It's a week before the prom, and you've just been dumped. When you show up with your last-minute date, your ex turns green. Does it feel:

❏ **Better**
❏ **Worse**

7. You had a great Valentine's Day with your steady, but apparently he didn't. The next day he dropped the bomb. You later found out he wanted to do it before V Day but held off to spare your feelings. Does that make it:

❏ **Better**
❏ **Worse**

8. The same babe dumped you twice. Like a bad cold, he's back again! You're not interested except for payback time. If you dated just to dump him, would you feel:

❏ **Better**
❏ **Worse**

9. Your hunk is sending signals that a dump is on the way! You bail first, not really wanting to. Does that make you feel:

❏ **Better**
❏ **Worse**

10. You both agree that things aren't right. He suggests a trial separation, not a dump. Do you feel:

❏ **Better**
❏ **Worse**

Scoring

I. You should feel better. You tried to make it work; you gave it time and you know his feelings weren't trashed. If at first you feel worse, it's only because any breakup hurts. At least you had the class to put in the extra effort.

2. Definitely better. You were brave enough to share something painful about yourself. Just because your crush ended, you are no less valuable as a friend. Everyone gets dumped sometime—just move on.

3. Maybe worse. You saved the cash, but you may wonder what he got for you! Next time don't base your relationship on gifts or saving money. Try for something deeper. Holidays are only once in a while; you have the rest of the year to worry about.

4. In the long run, worse. You can't be involved and escape the chance of being dumped. Love means risk, and you could be missing out on something great. You may feel better in the short term, but to tell the truth, you're really chickening out.

5. Both better and worse. At first it may make you feel better because your bud finally has experienced the same pain. But that will soon fade, and you'll feel compassion for your friend. She was there for you. Don't rub it in with "It's about time it happened to you." She knows.

6. Again, better and worse. You're glad your ex sees that you survived the breakup, but you're still a little bummed that you weren't there with him.

7. Overall, you should feel better. It was nice that he considered your feelings, but if you feel like you're an obligation, it's natural.

8. It might temporarily seem better—it's about time he felt the pain! Upon reflection, you realize that two wrongs don't make a right and that dropping him wouldn't erase the misery you experienced when dumped. Throw this guy back and keep your standards.

9. Worse! You let him control you. Plus, this dude didn't have the courage to come right out and tell you it's over; he let you do all the heavy lifting. You lost both ways. Next time stick to your emotions—if you lose, you lose, but at least you played the game fair.

10. Both. You feel worse because he formalized the dump, but afterward feel better because you're out of a sticky situation with no blood on your hands!

DUMP THERAPY:
How Do I Get Over Him?

Ouch! Although getting dumped can feel like the worst pain in the world, heartbreak is curable and you *will* be happy again. Meanwhile, if you've gone into crush cardiac arrest and need some TLC, try taking our quiz along with a soothing mug of hot chocolate! Indicate which of these would be a positive love cure and which would be a negative dumb and dumber way of prolonging your torment.

	Positive	Negative
1. Keeping trusted buds close	____	____
2. A three-week food binge	____	____
3. Making of list of everything you hate about him, then throwing it away	____	____
4. Making a list of everything you hate about him, then e-mailing it to all your buds	____	____
5. Helping out with a community event	____	____
6. Starting a new hobby	____	____
7. Crying every day for a month	____	____
8. Improving your grades	____	____
9. Letting your bod go blimpo	____	____
10. Rereading his notes and cards	____	____

	Positive	Negative
11. Keeping up his shrine in your locker	____	____
12. Getting more exercise	____	____
13. Giving yourself one week to cry it out	____	____
14. Believing he's the only guy for you	____	____
15. Playing the songs you both loved	____	____
16. Writing your thoughts and feelings in a diary	____	____
17. Telling as many girls as possible not to go out with him	____	____
18. Keeping it all bottled up and pretending nothing happened	____	____
19. Making out with the next dude to come along— even if you don't like him	____	____
20. Sending him anguished, bitter letters	____	____
21. Driving by the ex's house constantly	____	____
22. Pretending you dumped him	____	____
23. Joining a new club	____	____
24. Treating yourself to a calming herbal bath	____	____
25. Going out to new events	____	____

Scoring

1. Positive	10. Negative	19. Negative
2. Negative	11. Negative	20. Negative
3. Positive	12. Positive	21. Negative
4. Negative	13. Positive	22. Negative
5. Positive	14. Negative	23. Positive
6. Positive	15. Negative	24. Positive
7. Negative	16. Positive	25. Positive
8. Positive	17. Negative	
9. Negative	18. Negative	

If you got most correct:
Moving On!

Your love life has thrown you a curveball, but after an appropriate period of mourning, you're up and running. You're secure enough to know lots of other hunks will come along—and they will.

Mostly wrong answers:
Crying Game.

Your ex is gone, so stop beating up on yourself. Saying bad things about him only makes you feel worse. The world is loaded with mega-babes waiting to love you. Just get back out where you can be seen.

Can You Cure the
BREAKUP BLUES?

After a breakup, you're probably heading for the nearest Baskin Robbins. Even if the split was your idea, you can still be bummed because your romance didn't work out. Look on the bright side, though. You're not stuck with Mr. Wrong, so that frees you up to meet somebody else who's way better. Right now, girl, you need to find inner peace. Check out this quiz to see how good you are at comforting yourself.

I. **You want to date others. When you tell your steady, he goes ballistic and calls you horrible names. How do you handle this?**

   A Decide all guys are treacherous and vow never to date again.

   B Put out the word he's psycho.

   C Tell your buds you feel bad, let them console you, and finally laugh about it.

2. **Last weekend everything was wonderful. Then he met Whitney, and before you could say "dump," it was over. What would make you feel better?**

   A Stay home from school for a week.

   B Put out the word that he was a lousy lover.

   C Have a good cry, then go out with the buds.

3. The prom is a month away. When you bring it up with your steady, he's evasive. Finally he tells you right out he doesn't want to go with you. How do you handle this blow?

  A Turn down any invitations you may get and mope at home.

  B Tell everybody he dumped you right after you bought an expensive gown so he looks extra bad.

  C Do something gorge for yourself: new makeup, a phat sweater, a trip to the salon. You'll radiate confidence and attract other guys.

4. You really felt you had something *soooo* special with your crush. Then you learned he was unfaithful and you broke it off. But you can't shake the memories of the good, close times. How do you move on?

  A Daydream about him constantly.

  B Write him a long, angry letter and e-mail it, with copies to all your friends.

  C Tell yourself that if you found something good with this guy, you'll find it with another.

5. Friday night you delivered the blow. What will make Saturday night feel less guilty?

  A A quart of rocky road ice cream.

  B A long sob session with the ex's friends.

  C A movie with your buds.

6. **For months you dreamed of landing this crush. After three heavenly dates, it's over. How long should you be in mourning?**
   A Weeks, possibly months.
   B Until you tell everybody in school what a creep he is.
   C The warranty on this relationship ran out fast. Start looking for a new guy.

7. **Lunchtime, he told you good-bye. Now you've got to face his crush shrine in your locker. What would make you feel better:**
   A Leaving it up another month—he could come back.
   B Throwing all his things on the hallway floor.
   C Taking it down after school and throwing it in the garbage. After all, you have to make room for the next crush.

8. **You went fifty-fifty on your favorite CDs. After the breakup, he wants his share. Would it soothe your bruised feelings to:**
   A Refuse.
   B Throw them on your front lawn.
   C Return them right away—via his best bud.

9. **You're both on the yearbook committee. Tomorrow you have to face him for the first time since he pulled the plug. Would it make you feel better to:**
   A Plunge him into an ice bath.
   B Argue with everything he proposes.
   C Act the same way you always do. In fact, shoot him a smile every now and then to let him know nothing's bothering you.

10. You have to face Mom and Dad with the news you broke it off with your long-term steady. Would it help you to:

A Pretend it meant nothing.
B Bad-mouth your ex with personal details.
C Let them know you're blue so they can comfort you.

Scoring

Mostly As: Cry Me a River! You're going to wallow in it—and the only one who will suffer will be you. Certainly, you should never show a guy how much he has hurt you, because that feeds his ego at the cost of yours. Act as through he didn't even land a punch; that will let some of the air out of his tires.

Mostly Bs: Psycho Bitch! You might want to head for the nearest shrink's couch because, girl, you are one angry person. You're way possessive and that's making you vindictive. Let go—do some running or go out, but ditch those ideas of revenge if you want to be happy in the long run.

Mostly Cs: Heart Smart. You're really on target. Not only do you know how to take care of yourself, but you know the truth about the downside of love— that heartbreak needs TLC to mend, not shock therapy. Being extra good to yourself now means a shorter, healthier recovery period.

CHAPTER TWO

THE BUD REPORT
What's Good ... What's Bad?

Been buds forever? Or just since you moved? Is your best bud moving? How will you deal with that? And what about a bud who's sometimes fickle or worse after your hunk? Or a bud who's so sweet, it makes you want to be a better friend. Whether blading, wolfing down pizza, sharing secrets, or crush spotting, a girl needs a bud. Not only is a good bud another pair of eyes (she'll help you scope 'em out!), she's a shoulder to cry on and a hand to hold when times get rough.

Yes, a teen chick has to have good buds. Are you totally bringing out the best in your bud and vice versa? Take these tests to be sure.

Are Your **Friends** True?

You've always been loyal to your buds, but lately you've had some doubts about them. It's important people trust each other... so take this quiz to see how good you are at reading loyalty into situations.

1. **When blading with your buds, you are most likely to be:**
   - A holding hands and singing show tunes.
   - B skating five feet behind them because they asked to have a word alone.
   - C trying to catch your breath. They're better skaters than you.

2. **While shopping you find a dress you're crazy about. Your friends:**
   - A tell you how good it looks and want you to buy it.
   - B say, "Your butt looks *soooo* big! I can't believe you would wear that."
   - C say, "It looks fine. Can we go now?"

3. **It's Saturday night and it's a GNO (Girls Night Out). You all jump on the sofa. You sit:**
   - A between everyone. You always make the jokes that crack the gang up.
   - B on the floor—they wouldn't make room for you on the sofa.
   - C it doesn't matter. As long as you're with your friends.

4. You're really struggling with softball. Your friends tell you:

A not to feel bad. You just need some practice.

B they'll come over to help you every day.

C "You stink. Stay home."

5. You and your boyfriend (of six fabulous months) broke up yesterday—and are you bummed! Your friends:

A stick with you, then tell the nasty rumors he's been spreading about you.

B hang with your ex after school. He needs comforting, too.

C cheer you up by asking you over.

6. You're in a stall in the school bathroom when your friends walk in. You can't help hearing them:

A talk about what a great time they had at your sleepover.

B say how cute your boyfriend is and that you don't deserve him.

C Openly dish the latest gossip about you.

7. You're psyched about the concert you and the buds are going to. At the last minute their crushes invite them to a party. They:

A ditch you.

B go with you but complain the entire evening.

C go and have fun. They can see their crushes tomorrow.

8. Your friends are supposed to give you a ride home, but they forget. What do they do when they remember?

A Call you.

B Come and get you.

C Figure you can take care of yourself.

9. The guy you've been crushing on for months asks you out. Your friends:

A come over with their makeup and jewelry.

B are bitter and don't answer the phone.

C call you and say, "Have a great time."

10. It's time for a ride home. The car fits four, and you're number five. Your friends:

A flip you a quarter to call your mom.

B drop everyone else off and come back for you.

C all squeeze. You don't mind being closer.

Scoring

1. A-3, B-1, C-2
2. A-3, B-1, C-2
3. A-3, B-1, C-2
4. A-2, B-3, C-1
5. A-2, B-1, C-3
6. A-3, B-1, C-2
7. A-1, B-2, C-3
8. A-2, B-3, C-1
9. A-3, B-1, C-2
10. A-1, B-2, C-3

Your Score

**1 to 10: Start Shopping.
Your friends don't appreciate
you.** Before moving on, you could
talk to them about your feelings.
Maybe you're having some
miscommunications.

11 to 19: Watch Out.
Your friends are not
always there for you.
They're the kind who
skip out when some-
thing "better" comes up.

20 to 30: Best Buds.
You're lucky to have
friends like these. Hold
on to them; they're true.

COPYCAT FRIENDS:
do you have a TWIN?

Your best bud is great, but lately you've noticed that the two of you are more like twins than friends. Maybe it is because she bought the same jeans or sweater. Maybe you just like the same things, but read this to find out if she is trying to clone you or if you're just imagining seeing double. Check Y or N after each question.

I. You and your bud went for manicures. Did you get nail polish in exactly the same color? **Y__ N__**

2. You wanted to get your hair cut for the upcoming school year. You decide on a hip bob, even if it means chopping off all your luscious locks. Next week, does your friend show up with your new do? **Y__ N__**

3. While cruising around town, have you been mistaken for sisters? **Y__ N__**

4. For twins? **Y__ N__**

5. While shopping, does she always buy the same things you do and always ask for your opinion on everything? **Y__ N__**

6. Before doing anything, even going to the grocery store, does she check with you to see if you want to go? **Y__ N__**

7. You've picked up tap dancing. Does she sign up, too? **Y__ N__**

8. You buy the new trendy striped flip-flops. Does she get a pair?
Y___ N___

9. You want to buy a shirt offered in ten different colors. They're all nice, but you like the pretty purple one. When she picks a color to get, is it purple?
Y___ N___

10. You tell her you dig the new hottie at school. She hasn't stopped talking about him and how well she knows him ever since.
Y___ N___

11. You're crazy for the new hot flick in town. The day it comes out on video you buy it. Next time you step in her room, is there a poster of the movie's star on her wall?
Y___ N___

12. It's Saturday night, and you really want to hang with your boyfriend. Does she tag along?
Y___ N___

13. You get voted editor of the yearbook. Does she join the committee? Coincidence?
Y___ N___

14. You made up your own cool word like "phat" or "fly." Does she start using it 24/7?
Y___ N___

15. You get invited to an A-list party. Does she invite herself?
Y___ N___

Your Score

1 to 5 yes answers: You are just great friends with a lot in common, like similar interests in clothing and boys. Don't worry, you are lucky to have such a cool friend. Take any similarities as flattering.

6 to 9 yes answers: Possible Clone. You need to really think about whether she is copying you or just clinging. You have some of the same interests, but she needs to realize that you need your own space, too. Talk to her if you feel trapped.

10 to 15 yes answers: Total Clone. Get a grip. Calm down and talk to her. She needs her own identity, not yours. Pay attention to her actions. If they are bothering you, do something. If not, you will just fill up with frustration and explode with anger later on.

old friends vs. new:
WHICH ARE BETTER?

You've known them since kindergarten, you're practically sisters. They've always come to your rescue and made you feel good. But you also love your new buds, too. Who's the better gal pal, old or new?

1. You feel more "yourself" around?
❑ OLD ❑ NEW

2. You would more likely tell your secrets to?
❑ OLD ❑ NEW

3. You feel as close as sisters with?
❑ OLD ❑ NEW

4. They are the "in" crowd?
❑ OLD ❑ NEW

5. You just got dumped. You'll most likely cry to whom tonight?
❑ OLD ❑ NEW

6. It's Saturday night and you're bored. You call?
❑ OLD ❑ NEW

7. Ten years from now you'll be in touch with?
❑ OLD ❑ NEW

8. You'd rather spend a week on vacation with?
❑ OLD ❑ NEW

9. You are at summer camp and down to your last stamp. You write to?
❑ OLD ❑ NEW

10. You leave for school tomorrow. You cram some last-minute time in with?

❏ OLD ❏ NEW

11. You met the guy of your dreams. Whom do you tell?

❏ OLD ❏ NEW

12. Whom do you feel more comfortable boy-sighting with?

❏ OLD ❏ NEW

Your Score

OLD OR NEW? Which did you check more of? Was it a tie, or close? Sure, you have spent mega more time with your old buds, but maybe you're ready for some new additions. Just because you don't hang with the same exact clique 24/7 doesn't mean that anything is wrong. Bringing new faces into the group can be a blast. But remember, while it's always good to meet new people, you have to treat your old buds well all the time.

are you a terrific best friend ?

From e-mail messages to late-night calls, your best bud is always there for you. You share everything with her—crush sightings, classes, clothes, secrets, and more. She's cool, but are you being the absolute best friend you can? Take the Best Bud Test to learn if you're as solid a pal as you could be.

I. My bud failed her Latin test, so I help her study for the next one.
❏ TRUE
❏ FALSE

2. I always tell her any mean rumors I hear about her.
❏ TRUE
❏ FALSE

3. If my bud tries a new sport, I go to her games.
❏ TRUE
❏ FALSE

4. I always listen to her family problems and try to help.
❏ TRUE
❏ FALSE

5. My bud's parents take us out for dinner, but I don't have to thank them.
❏ TRUE
❏ FALSE

6. I help pay if she's broke.
❏ TRUE
❏ FALSE

7. I call her first with the latest dish.
❏ TRUE
❏ FALSE

8. After sleepovers, I leave before the cleanup.
❏ TRUE
❏ FALSE

9. If someone disses my bud, I blow them off.
❏ TRUE
❏ FALSE

10. I often forget to return her things, but it's okay, right?
❏ TRUE
❏ FALSE

11. If she has to baby-sit her little brother, I hang out with her.
❏ TRUE
❏ FALSE

12. If she says she'll call me right back, I get on the phone with my other buds for hours anyway.
❏ TRUE
❏ FALSE

13. If I want to get in with the cool kids, I can always dump on her.
❏ TRUE
❏ FALSE

14. When a crush dumps my bud, I try to cheer her up.
❏ TRUE
❏ FALSE

15. I make sure she's invited to parties.
❏ TRUE
❏ FALSE

16. If I'm supposed to go out with her, but something better comes up, I ditch her.
❏ TRUE
❏ FALSE

17. If I break something of hers, I don't tell her.
❏ TRUE
❏ FALSE

18. When my bud's stomach is growling, I share my food with her.
❏ TRUE
❏ FALSE

19. If my bud and I are having a rough patch and her feelings are hurt, I wait until it blows over before calling.
❏ TRUE
❏ FALSE

20. When we get together, sometimes she decides what to do, sometimes I do.
❏ TRUE
❏ FALSE

21. I went on her family vacation with her. We had a ball and made up fast after a fight.
❏ TRUE
❏ FALSE

22. We once had a fight and didn't talk for a week. Then I called her.
❏ TRUE
❏ FALSE

23. Even though my best bud's family moved away for a year-long sabbatical, I keep in touch with letters and cards.
❏ TRUE
❏ FALSE

24. If I'm depressed, I call her up and talk until she's depressed, too.
❏ TRUE
❏ FALSE

25. Even if my bud does something stupid, I give her a hug and get on with it.
❏ TRUE
❏ FALSE

Scoring

1. True	6. True	11. True	16. False	21. True
2. False	7. True	12. False	17. False	22. True
3. True	8. False	13. False	18. True	23. True
4. True	9. True	14. True	19. False	24. False
5. False	10. False	15. True	20. True	25. True

Your Score

1 to 5 right answers: Friend-Less.

You're lucky to even have friends. Better start being a little more giving and sign up for some loyalty lessons now.

5 to 10 right answers: Get Friendly.

Don't be so tight with the love. The more you give your friends, the more fun you'll have, too. Loosen up.

10 to 15 right answers: Friends-R-U.

You could turn into top-notch friend material. Think about what you could do to be more sympathetic and understanding.

15 to 20 right answers: First Rate Friend!

You're everything a friend could ask for, and probably your best friend knows it. She's lucky!

is your bud good to you?

You like to spend your free time with your bud, but sometimes you realize that she disappoints you. Take this quiz to see how true your bud is to you.

1. **You leave a message on your friend's machine for her to call you back so you can go to the beach the next day. You hear from her:**

   A the next evening. She says she didn't think it was a good beach day, so why bother to call you back?

   B in an hour, and she is sooo psyched to hit the sand.

   C late that night. She felt that it was more important to answer her other messages before she called you.

2. **Your bud comes over, and when a guy you've both been crushing on calls, she happens to answer the phone. Then she tells you:**

   A to leave the room, they have to talk alone.

   B that it's him and gives you the phone.

   C that you can stay, but don't speak because she doesn't want him to know that you're in the room.

3. You're at the town carnival with your friend when she sees that hottie she's been cruising. She starts flirting with him, then:

 A tells you that they are going for a walk and will be back in five minutes, but you don't see her for hours.

 B tells him that you and she are going on the Ferris wheel and invites him along.

 C points out another friend of yours, hoping the two of you will go on without her.

4. Your bud is at your house talking on the phone when you get a message to call another friend back. Your bud:

 A tells you that she is talking about something more important and makes you wait a half hour for the phone.

 B tells the person she is talking to that she has to get off the phone (after all, it is your house).

 C gets off the phone, but stares at her watch the whole time you're talking, then grabs it back the second that you hang up.

5. You're getting together later for a movie with your best bud. The show starts at nine o'clock. She picks you up at:

 A quarter after nine, saying you can always catch the late show.

 B seven and helps you pick out something nice to wear in case you run into any cute guys.

 C quarter to nine after you have been pacing the boards for twenty minutes worrying you'll be late.

6. **In the school cafeteria, you cruise over to the crowded lunch table where your best friend is sitting. You're really excited because you want to tell her about the bio quiz you just aced. She:**

    A points out the table is full, and besides, you can tell her later about the quiz.

    B pulls over a chair for you even though space is tight plus she's very happy when you tell her about the quiz.

    C helps you find another table and sits with you for a minute while you tell her your news. When you're done she goes back to her table and you don't see her for the rest of the lunch period.

7. **When you and your friend are shopping at the mall she spends all her money. She asks to borrow money to:**

    A buy a dress. After all, she might let you borrow it when she is sick of it.

    B never. She knows that you work hard for your money.

    C pay for parking, even though she drove and you always pay when you drive.

8. **Earlier you shared a hot piece of gossip with your bud about Susie, the clan goody-goody. After swearing your bud to secrecy, later you heard:**

    A her telling the story to a group she wants to get in with.

    B zipsky! She doesn't want to be busted.

    C that Susie thought you started the rumor.

9. **The class geek keeps calling you up because:**

   A your bud had her family say she was hanging out with you so she could shake him.

   B someone told him you like him.

   C he's your new study partner.

10. **Once you went everywhere with your bud. Now she has dropped you like dry ice because "her new friends don't know you." Is she:**

    A completely disloyal.

    B fickle and immature.

    C all of the above.

Your Score

Mostly As: On the Down Side. Even though you are devoted to her, it looks as though she isn't devoted to you. She constantly disappoints you. Try looking for a friend who will treat you the way you deserve to be treated.

Mostly Bs: In Balance. It seems that you two are on the same level. You care about each other and enjoy your time together. This is the way friendship should be.

Mostly Cs: More to Come. You have to read the signals. Even though she goes slightly out of her way for you, you need more of a commitment from a good friend. Talk to her or look for someone who isn't just a user and a loser.

My Best Bud Hooked Up with My Guy!
KICK BUTT OR FORGIVE HER?

If there is one area that's strictly hands off, it's your crush zone. What would you do if suddenly it were invaded? And by your best bud? Do you forgive her or kick some serious bud butt? Check out these heart-breakers:

1. You hoped this crush was yours forever and told your bud how you felt.

___ YES
___ NO

2. She broke the news about hooking up with him.

___ YES
___ NO

3. She swears this one smooch session was the only time.

___ YES
___ NO

4. You had both been crushing on this hunk all year.

___ YES
___ NO

5. Your hot-lips "boy-friend" told your bud he only liked you as a friend before putting the moves on her.

___ YES
___ NO

6. You've been on again, off again with this crush for months.

___ YES
___ NO

THE TEEN QUIZ BOOK

7. Be honest . . . have you ever scoped out her crushes?

___ YES

___ NO

8. She swore it meant nothing to her.

___ YES

___ NO

9. And it was not a long lip-lock.

___ YES

___ NO

10. You ignored the hot rumors your crush was a player.

___ YES

___ NO

Scoring

1. Yes: If you told her how much you were crushing, you're entitled to feel betrayed.

No: If it was only in your head, how was your friend to know how much it meant?

2. Yes: Bonus points for her confessing. That had to be tough.

No: It's extra painful to hear it from someone else. Ask yourself: Did she have time to fess up before the e-mail went flying?

3. Yes: One hookup is not enough to ruin a deep friendship.

No: If they've been locking lips for a while, it's got to be awkward for you. Accept it or you'll lose both the boy and the bud.

4. Yes: If you didn't land him first, you can't blame her for trying.

No: She never told you she dug him? Or did she wait to see if you would land him?

5. Yes: Ouch! This hound should have let you know how he felt.

No: Ask yourself: Why did he make out with her? This two-timer is not good enough for you.

6. Yes: On-again, off-again relationships are too rocky to last; someone else was bound to nail him.

No: If you had been steadies, then your friend's betrayal would hurt more. And you may have to move on, maybe from both. Loyalty is something we can expect from our friends.

7. Yes: Okay, so you check out her guys. Maybe that's why you're buds—you like the same things.

No: Hmmm—never? You are a good friend.

8. Yes: Sometimes teens just want to make out—but it's no good if it's your guy.

No: If she really digs him and he digs her, it's doomed for you. You have no choice but to bow out gracefully if her friendship is important to you.

9. Yes: Long lip-lock or short—are you really this hung up on the details?

No: Call off the investigation and declare this case closed.

10. Yes: Girl, love is always Buyer Beware, and a player won't easily change.

No: Always read the "labels" carefully. Holding on to a teenage Casanova is virtually impossible.

your **best friend** is moving:
Are You a **Moper** or a **Coper?**

Not since Thelma hooked up with Louise have two friends clicked together like you and your bud. She knows your crush history, your horoscope, what you really want for your birthday. You've gone through rockin' times and sad, but nothing is worse than this— she's moving! What will life be like, will you survive? Take this quiz to see if you recognize the healthy ways to handle this blow.

Read each statement and check if it's a healthy or unhealthy way to cope.

		Healthy	Unhealthy
1.	If possible, I'll e-mail her.	_____	_____
2.	I'll always hate her parents.	_____	_____
3.	The day she leaves, down come all her photos . . . it's too sad.	_____	_____
4.	She'll send me photos of her new house and room.	_____	_____
5.	If our phone bills soar, I'll put some of my baby-sitting dough toward them.	_____	_____
6.	We plan to visit next vacation.	_____	_____

	Healthy	Unhealthy

7. I'll never get close to anyone again. ____ ____

8. Everybody else has a best friend. It's not fair I'll be so lonely. ____ ____

9. When she makes other friends, she'll think I'm nothing. ____ ____

10. I expect instant updates on all the cuties she meets. ____ ____

11. We'll spend part of the summer together. ____ ____

12. I'll surprise her by showing up for her family's Christmas party. ____ ____

13. We'll exchange copies of our high school yearbooks. ____ ____

14. I'll get her special stationery and lots of stamps so she can always write. ____ ____

15. I'll throw her a surprise going-away party. ____ ____

16. We're going to make videotapes of any parties we throw. ____ ____

17. We'll exchange phone calling cards so we can talk anywhere. ____ ____

18. I'm not going to bother to keep her in my photo album. ____ ____

	Healthy	Unhealthy
19. I'm going to stock the kitchen with loads of goodies to pig out on right after she leaves.	____	____
20. We'll do the same exercise work-out tape then compare notes.	____	____

Scoring

1. Healthy	6. Healthy	11. Healthy	16. Healthy
2. Unhealthy	7. Unhealthy	12. Healthy	17. Healthy
3. Unhealthy	8. Unhealthy	13. Healthy	18. Unhealthy
4. Healthy	9. Unhealthy	14. Healthy	19. Unhealthy
5. Healthy	10. Healthy	15. Healthy	20. Healthy

How did you do? If you agreed with us at least fifteen times, you're a coper. Having a best friend move away is a shock, but you'll always be buds if you both make an effort. The main thing is to accept the change, make the best of it, and not get twisted up and bitter.

If you disagreed with us more than five times, stop moping and start coping. It's up to you if you stay sad and weirded out, or if you cope with reality. Besides, your bud really needs you now—she's the one who's moving into strange territory. And deep down, she's probably scared. Help her out, and yourself too, by being more involved in making things better.

CHAPTER THREE

FEELING SUPER
The 411 on Health and Exercise

What's better: watching a track meet or running in one? Staying in shape or just thinking about it? Smart chicks know that it's the buff bods that get the looks. That doesn't mean super-thin, but healthy and toned. If people today are more into exercise and nutrition than ever before, shouldn't teens be, too? Or are teens going to let fifty-year-old moms run circles around them? As if!

Check out your food and exercise smarts with these quizzes. If you're not in top shape yet, don't panic and pig out. With a buff new outlook you soon will be.

howbuffareyou?

It's a guy thing—most of them notice a body that's toned and buff. Besides that, looking good says a lot of positive things about you. Are you doing your best to look great, or are you watching too many afternoon soaps? Find out if you're a pro or a couch potato.

You get home from school starving. Mostly likely you head for the:

- ❑ a) jumbo bag of chips (they'll calm your craving).
- ❑ b) handful of pretzels.
- ❑ c) water. You'll stick it out until dinner.

You wake up at eight on Saturday morning. You:

- ❑ a) wake up?
- ❑ b) get up and try out the new blades.
- ❑ c) go back to sleep for an hour then go for a light walk.

Your idea of a great afternoon exercise is:

- ❑ a) hitting the couch for the afternoon talk shows.
- ❑ b) playing some basketball with friends for an hour.
- ❑ c) riding your bike to the end of the driveway to get the mail.

4

How many seasonal sports do you play a year?

- ❑ a) does gym class count?
- ❑ b) all of them.
- ❑ c) a couple of intermurals once in a while during the winter.

Your role model most likely resembles:

- ❑ a) role model? Did you say hard roll?
- ❑ b) Gabrielle Reece.
- ❑ c) Ricki Lake.

You just finished gym class. You thirst for:

- ❑ a) chocolate milk.
- ❑ b) water.
- ❑ c) soda.

It's a rainy day. How do you get in your workout?

- ❑ a) promise yourself that you will do twice as much tomorrow.
- ❑ b) throw in a step video and feel the burn.
- ❑ c) put in your favorite CD and dance to a few songs.

Your friend invites you to the mall, but it's time for your workout. You:

- ❑ a) ditch the workout. You'd rather shop than sweat.
- ❑ b) ask if she'll wait an hour. You want to work out.
- ❑ c) speed-walk around the block to her house.

9 You're snowed in and out of milk. You:

❑ a) bag it and have soda instead.

❑ b) shovel the driveway and go out to get some.

❑ c) ask your neighbor for some.

10 You're at your best friend's birthday party. You've already pigged out on the cookies. You:

❑ a) forget about the cookies. They were a warm-up for the cake.

❑ b) go for the fruit salad.

❑ c) have a sliver of cake and promise yourself to do fifty extra sit-ups tonight.

Your Score

Mostly As: Couch Potato. You should dump your bag of chips and grab your blades. Gym class isn't enough if you are going to pig out every afternoon. Start out with a light run or swift walk every other day after school for half an hour. You'll feel better about yourself soon.

Mostly Bs: Fitness Pro. You have got it all right. You know the right combination of snacks and exercise. Keep up the good work.

Mostly Cs: On Your Way. Good attitude, but you need to establish better exercise and eating habits. For example, when you are hungry in the afternoon, have a light snack. If you don't eat in the afternoon, you'll probably eat too much at dinner.

who's your
Sports Role Model?

Do you play sports and model yourself after famous athletes? Take this quiz to find out who your role models are and what that means. Circle the name that comes closest to being who you want to be.

Gabrielle Reece	Michael Jordan	Katarina Witt
Rebecca Lobo	Wayne Gretsky	Kim Zmeskal
Summer Sanders	Joe Montana	Nancy Kerrigan
Bonnie Blair	Ken Griffey, Jr.	Kerri Strug

If you circled . . .

An athlete in the left column: You like the athlete who is well known, but not a superstar. You can probably relate more to these people than those who you see on every other TV commercial.

An athlete in the middle column: You go for the glitz. You admire these high-profile superstars for being the best in their sports.

An athlete in the right column: These athletes have the total package—performance, music, costume. People in this column are in what is called showy sports, like ice skating or gymnastics. You know they get criticized a lot, but you're loyal anyway.

what's your
snack
IQ? RATE THE FOODS

You try to eat healthy, but are you doing yourself more harm than good? Below is a list of some favorite snack foods. Rate them on a scale of 1 to 5 —1 being the worst for you, 5 the best. Then check your score to see if your nutrition know-how makes you a moron or a genius!

Peanut butter and banana ____

Sour cream and onion potato chips ____

Red delicious apple ____

Blueberry cereal bar ____

Ham sandwich with mayonnaise ____

Pasta ____

Chocolate bar ____

Cheese and crackers ____

Fruit ice pop ____

Watermelon ____

Cantaloupe ____

Cookies 'n' cream ice cream ____

Buttered bagel _____

Macaroni and cheese _____

Caesar salad _____

Raw vegetables and vinegar _____

Turkey breast with
lettuce and tomato on a roll _____

Bacon, egg, and cheese biscuit _____

Blueberries _____

Reduced-fat crackers _____

Strawberries _____

Scoring

Peanut butter and banana: 1. While the banana is healthful, the peanut butter is very high in both fat and calories.

Sour cream and onion potato chips: 1. High in calories and fat and not a lot of nutritional value.

Red Delicious apple: 5. A very good snack, lots of vitamins.

Blueberry cereal bar: 3. Some of these bars are good, no fat and low calories, but others aren't as good as you think. Be sure to read the labels.

Ham sandwich with mayonnaise: 1. What are you thinking! Ham can be a very fatty meat. Try turkey. Also, mayonnaise is very fatty and high in cholesterol (unless you use lowfat or light mayonnaise).

Pasta: 3. Good for energy because it is a carbo-hydrate, but not a lot of nutritional value. Be careful not to load up on butter; try a little tomato sauce.

Chocolate bar: 2. Chocolate is high in fat. If you eat the whole thing you are really hurting yourself.

Cheese and crackers: 3. The crackers are good and a little cheese is okay because every person needs a little fat in her diet. Just don't put too much cheese on the crackers.

Fruit ice pop: 3. You probably think that this snack is great because the pop is low in fat and calories and has fruit in it. But not all fruit pops are made with real fruits, so you might be filling up with a lot of artificial ingredients. Try an all-natural one or a piece of real fruit.

Watermelon: 5. Watermelon is flavorful and filling (all that water). It also has lots of vitamin A.

Cantaloupe: 5. Cantaloupe contains potassium and vitamins A and C. These help wounds heal quicker.

Cookies 'n' cream ice cream: 1. Ice cream has a lot of fat and calories and the cookie contains additional animal fat.

Buttered bagel: 2. The bagel is good, but butter is fatty. Try some jelly instead.

Macaroni and cheese: 1. This is a fatty snack. There is usually butter, milk, and cheese in the sauce.

Caesar salad: 3. The salad is a great idea, but the dressing is high in both fat and calories. These days there are lowfat and nonfat dressings, so try one of those.

Raw vegetables and vinegar: 5. Keep up the good work. The vegetables are great sources of vitamins and the vinegar is a good alternative to fatty dressings.

Turkey breast with lettuce and tomato on a roll: 5. This is a great snack. Turkey is a good cold cut, one of the lowest in fat, and the lettuce and tomato are great ways to liven up the sandwich.

Bacon, egg, and cheese biscuit: 1. One of the worst things you could put in your body. Every element in this snack is extremely high in fat, calories, and cholesterol.

Blueberries: 5. A great idea for an on-the-run snack.

Reduced-fat crackers: 4. You are doing a good job! These days many snacks come in a reduced-fat form and still taste good.

Strawberries: 5. Strawberries contain many vitamins.

Your Score

If you got **15 or more** of these foods right, you really know what you are doing.

If you got **between 10 and 15** right, try to learn more about what you eat so you can form smarter eating habits.

If you got **below 10** right answers, you are in the unenlightened category. Remember, a healthy body is usually a good-looking body. Learn to eat right for that if nothing else!

what's your
Exercise know-how?

If you're buffing up for the beach or training for team tryouts, you'll be better off knowing more about exercise—what helps your body and what hurts it. Stretch your mental powers to a new high and see if you can score 100 on this Exercise Know-how Decathlon. Circle the answers you think are right.

Event 1 (worth 5 points)

Soccer is a great sport for teens because:
a. it provides aerobic benefits.
b. you get cool uniforms.

Event 2 (worth 10 points)

Which is better before a workout?
a. a sweetened drink.
b. a glass of orange juice.

Event 3 (worth 10 points)

You should warm up before exercising because:
a. muscles stretch more easily after warming up.
b. you want to use up as much time as possible.

Event 4 (worth 10 points)

After-exercise stretching, or cooling down, can help your body feel better because:

a. it keeps you moving.

b. it increases flexibility.

Event 5 (worth 5 points)

If you join Mom for a walking workout, you should swing your arms because:

a. it looks cool.

b. you will get an upper-body workout.

Event 6 (worth 15 points)

Finding the right exercise shoes is important because the wrong ones will:

a. hurt your feet and cause muscle fatigue.

b. wear out fast.

Event 7 (worth 5 points)

If you're jogging when it's humid, you must:

a. stop for ice cream.

b. drink lots of water.

Event 8 (worth 15 points)

Wearing a sturdy bicycle helmet is essential because:

a. you're required to.

b. it will protect you from serious head injuries.

Event 9 (worth 15 points)

When swimming you should vary your strokes in the beginning of your workout in order to:

a. burn up calories.

b. give all your muscles a chance to warm up.

Event 10 (worth 10 points)

Weight training is beneficial for women because it:

a. helps you meet hunky guys.

b. tones your body, increases circulation, and beefs up your bones.

SCORING

1. a	4. b	7. b	10. b
2. b	5. b	8. b	
3. a	6. a	9. b	

Your Score

If you scored 60 to 75 points: BRONZE. Stay informed and in shape. Reading up on what's good for your body makes exercise more interesting and effective.

75 to 90 points: SILVER: You're polishing up your athletic act to a gleaming shine. Keep on working out and you'll feel as good as you look.

90 to 100 points: GOLD. Thanks to mental work-outs, your brains are as buff as your bod. Stay on top of exercise and nutrition trends and you'll stay in top shape.

can you read the
"Time To Buff Up" Signals?

A Buff-Up Alert can happen at any time of year, not just when bikini days approach. If lately you've been sensing there's a little more to you than maybe you would like, such as a pneumatic mid-section (!), it could be time to get serious. Take this test to see if your Buff-Up Meter matches ours, then spring into action to get that hot bod! Rate from 1 to 3 points how true to you the following statements are:

1 = Never to rarely
2 = Occasionally
3 = Okay, it's true

1. For months now, your uniform has been over-sized t-shirts and baggy pants. _____

2. When you put your arms next to your sides, you're surprised by your bulk. _____

3. When you sit down, it's getting harder to cross your legs comfortably. _____

4. When shopping in the mall, you're bummed out by your image in the dressing room mirrors. _____

5. The saleslady automatically brought you clothes two sizes larger than you used to wear. _____

6. In the swimsuit department, you head for the one-piece section. _____

7. Mom's been thinking about borrowing *your* clothes. _____

8. You love to go to the movies because of the candy counter. _____

9. Lately, you don't want anyone to touch you because he might think you're fat. _____

10. The ice cream truck automatically stops at your home. _____

11. Halloween is your favorite holiday. _____

12. You're starting to envy anyone in really good shape. _____

13. Anything in Lycra scares you. _____

14. You rarely take the stairs. _____

15. You mute the TV when weight-loss ads come on. _____

16. You can't remember the last time you bought hot underwear. _____

17. June, July, and August are the cruelest months of the year. _____

18. You glimpsed the reflection of a heavy person in a shop window—and it was you! _____

19. Your wardrobe consists almost entirely of dark colors. _____

20. You haven't used your exercise equipment in the past six months. _____

21. The longest vegging-out session you had lasted over a month. _____

Your Score

21 to 30 points: **Buffed-Up Babe!**

Sounds as though you're in great shape, mentally and otherwise. You may have the occasional lapse, but your head and habits are soooo healthy. You must look super!

31 to 45 points: **On Your Way.**

Buffing up means regular workouts and smart eating. Buff up your brain, too, by learning all you can about nutrition; you'll form good eating habits for life. Psych yourself up by working out with a bud.

46 to 63 points: **Shape It Up, Baby!**

Get out those blades! Okay, you were brave and took this test, now take the next step and free yourself from those down attitudes. Continued exercise and a good eating plan will help you get that buff bod. Remember—no extremes. No crash diets that leave you regaining your lost weight. You've got the rest of your life to look good, and you can start now.

what's the **dish** on EATING RIGHT?

Wish you ate just because you're hungry? You can because good food is loaded with vitamins and nutrients to make you strong and healthy, plus feel full so you don't pig out. What do you know about eating smart? Quiz yourself below.

1. Organic food is free from pesticides.
❑ **TRUE**
❑ **FALSE**

2. All vegetables should be thoroughly washed before eating.
❑ **TRUE**
❑ **FALSE**

3. The Food Guide Pyramid recommends one serving of vegetables a day.
❑ **TRUE**
❑ **FALSE**

4. Peas, beans, nuts, eggs, fish, and meat all contain protein.
❑ **TRUE**
❑ **FALSE**

5. Vitamin A helps maintain healthy skin, hair, nails, and teeth.
❑ **TRUE**
❑ **FALSE**

6. You can't take too many vitamins.
❑ **TRUE**
❑ **FALSE**

7. Breakfast is the least important meal of the day.
❑ TRUE
❑ FALSE

8. White bread is as good a source of fiber as whole-grain bread.
❑ TRUE
❑ FALSE

9. The skin on chicken tastes good and is good for you.
❑ TRUE
❑ FALSE

10. Salad dressings are usually high in fat.
❑ TRUE
❑ FALSE

11. A chef salad containing whole eggs, ham, cheese, and olives is a lowfat meal.
❑ TRUE
❑ FALSE

12. A vegetable pizza is a better snack than pepperoni pizza.
❑ TRUE
❑ FALSE

13. The carbohydrates food group includes cereal, bread, and grains.
❑ TRUE
❑ FALSE

14. Air-popped popcorn is a better snack than tortilla chips.
❑ TRUE
❑ FALSE

15. Calcium develops healthy bones, which is important for teens.
❑ TRUE
❑ FALSE

16. Eating candy will give you an energy boost.
❑ TRUE
❑ FALSE

17. It's not important to read the labels on foods.
❏ **TRUE**
❏ **FALSE**

18. Lose weight quickly if you want to keep it off.
❏ **TRUE**
❏ **FALSE**

19. Fried shrimp is good for you. After all, it's fish.
❏ **TRUE**
❏ **FALSE**

20. Snacking while you're talking on the phone doesn't really count.
❏ **TRUE**
❏ **FALSE**

Answers:

1. True. Organic food is supposed to be pesticide-free.

2. True. To be totally safe, all vegetables should be thoroughly scrubbed or rinsed.

3. False. We need 3 to 5 servings of vegetables, 6 to 11 servings of cereal, breads, grains, and grain products, and 2 to 4 servings of fruit.

4. True. Children and teens need 2 to 3 servings of protein a day to grow and develop strong bones and nails, muscles, shiny hair, and glowing skin.

5. True. Vitamin A is found in dairy products, deep yellow and orange veggies, oranges, and yellow fruits.

6. False. Every day our bodies need the vitamins and minerals found in a balanced diet. Overdosing with supplements can cause side effects.

7. False. A healthy breakfast stimulates alertness and helps you ace those early A.M. exams.

8. False. Whole-grain bread is a great source of good-for-you fiber, which helps keep your digestive track working.

9. False. Chicken skin is loaded with fat! Beware of not-so-hidden calories and toss most of it.

10. True. Mayonnaise is almost all fat. Try making your own using lowfat yogurt or buying lowfat dressings in the store.

11. False. Chef's salad can be very high in fat. Just because something is called a salad doesn't automatically mean it's lowfat.

12. True. There's less fat, sodium, and cholesterol in a pizza without pepperoni.

13. True. Carbohydrates are essential to healthy, slim bodies.

14. True. Air-popped popcorn is very low in fat and high in fiber.

15. True. Teens especially need calcium because their bodies are growing.

16. False. The sugar in candy may give you a rush but the feeling quickly disappears. A better snack is a bagel or hard roll.

17. False. It's super-important to know what you're putting in your body. Many foods are sky-high in sodium and hidden fats. Don't assume that because it's lowfat, it's low in calories.

18. False. Losing weight slowly by eating right and working out is the best way to keep it off.

19. False. The coating on fried foods soaks up fat. Remove it completely before eating or, better yet, order boiled shrimp.

20. False. Pay attention when you eat. Being distracted often makes a person eat more and remember it less.

CHAPTER FOUR

ACTING COOL
How You Handle Yourself

Have you raised whining to an art form? Do you have the endurance to outcomplain any of your buds? Do you have any buds? Are you one of those teens who think they're the planet around which everything orbits? We've all known bores like that—the kind of teen who thinks she's so special, we should thank her for taking advantage of us.

No, we think you're probably totally cool—brainy, considerate, and secure. In fact we know you are, and we hope you enjoy taking these tests that'll reveal more about majorly smart ways you handle yourself.

SINGLED OUT.
Are You Good at Dealing With Being Alone?

All your pals decided to try out for the play, and everyone made it. That is, everyone except you. Maybe it was just bad luck, but when you didn't make the soccer team either, you got down on yourself. Just because you didn't make the squad doesn't mean that your life is over. Take the quiz to find out if you are okay with being singled out. Check "Me" or "Not Me" as the situation applies.

1. It's Friday night, and all your friends are out on dates. Instead of sitting home, you decide to get up and go to the movies.
Me____   Not Me____

2. Although you're bummed you didn't make the cut for the team, you're satisfied underneath because you know you gave it all you had.
Me____   Not Me____

3. All your pals won their positions on student government. When you lost, you decided to throw in your towel and let them do the work.
Me____   Not Me____

4. You and the girls studied together for the final, but when everyone aced it and you got a C, did you get bitter with them?

Me___   Not Me___

5. All your pals are in the same PE class. Whenever it's time to grab partners, they link up and scram, leaving you alone. Do you grab a new face and make a friend?

Me___   Not Me___

Your Score

1. If you answered "Me," good for you for getting up and getting out of your house! Don't take showing up at the theater alone as embarrassing—at least you won't have to worry about your buddies eating your popcorn. If you answered "Not Me," try going. If you find that you don't like it, you can always go back home or hit the diner.

2. If you said "Me," bonus point for you. Obviously you're going to be a little down for not making the team, but at least you know that you put in 110 percent effort. And maybe now that you have all that spare time on your hands, you can get a job to make some extra cash. For the ones who answered "Not Me," ask if you can be the team manager or water girl. If you said "Not Me" because you didn't try your hardest, then you already know what you have to do.

3. If you said "Me," you are taking things a little too personally. So you didn't get voted in—that doesn't mean you can't help anyway. Plus, if you do help out, you'll get noticed and next time have a better chance of being elected. If you answered "Not Me," good for you. Now go put yourself on the list to help out on the homecoming float.

4. If you said "Me" and were a little bitter, that's normal—especially if you put in the same time studying. But were you listening to music or watching television while you were cramming? Those distractions may have made the difference. If you said "Not Me," congratulations for being mature. But you may want to find out what the problem was.

5. If you boldly answered "Me," great job! Not only have you turned a sticky situation into a good one, but you made a new friend in the meantime. For the "Not Me" readers, what did you do? You had to pair up with someone. Make life a positive experience, not something to get bent out of shape about.

are you a **DAY** person or a **NIGHT** person?

Y ou love staying up late at parties, but does that make you a night owl? Or is sunrise when you're most rockin' even though by eight P.M. you're out of it? Check out these symptoms to find out whether you're made for the day or live for the night.

Check true for the situations that are true for you and false for those that aren't.

1. You had a typical Friday night. On Saturday morning, you get up after ten.
❑ **TRUE**
❑ **FALSE**

2. You love the sunrise much more than the sunset.
❑ **TRUE**
❑ **FALSE**

3. You have to get in shape, but you want to beat the heat. You plan to run early in the morning, rather than after dinner.
❑ **TRUE**
❑ **FALSE**

4. You save your home-work until nine P.M. You can make it past mid-night before yawning.
❑ **TRUE**
❑ **FALSE**

5. You want to catch the news. You tune in at eleven P.M.
❑ TRUE
❑ FALSE

6. Your favorite meal of the day is breakfast.
❑ TRUE
❑ FALSE

7. In school you're most alert after lunch.
❑ TRUE
❑ FALSE

8. Late-night babysitting is a cinch.
❑ TRUE
❑ FALSE

9. Getting up early on vacations is something you normally do.
❑ TRUE
❑ FALSE

10. When the sun goes down, your spirits go up.
❑ TRUE
❑ FALSE

11. You schedule most of your heavy classes for the morning.
❑ TRUE
❑ FALSE

12. Ten P.M. is not too late to call your buds.
❑ TRUE
❑ FALSE

13. Your favorite movie time is nine P.M.
❑ TRUE
❑ FALSE

14. Getting up early for trips and vacations never throws you.
❑ TRUE
❑ FALSE

15. When someone says, "Meet me early in the morning," you think they mean before ten A.M.
❑ TRUE
❑ FALSE

16. You arrive at school knowing what's happening in the world because you've had the time to read the newspaper or catch the news on TV.
❑ TRUE
❑ FALSE

17. Daylight savings time agrees with you.
❑ TRUE
❑ FALSE

18. You start to get hungry for dinner at around eight o'clock.
❑ TRUE
❑ FALSE

19. You always catch *Saturday Night Live.*
❑ TRUE
❑ FALSE

20. Bankers' hours seem normal to you.
❑ TRUE
❑ FALSE

Your Score

True on 2, 3, 6, 9, 11, 14, 15, 16, 17, and 20:
Morning Glory! You love to get up early and get things done. Also, you probably accomplish more because waking up early gives you more time to do things your own way. Other advantages are the privacy and peacefulness you can only find in the morning.

True on 1, 4, 5, 7, 8, 10, 12, 13, 18, and 19:
Captain Midnight! You love going out late and sleeping past noon. You might be thought of as something of a procrastinator since you save your work for late at night. You'd rather watch the sunset than get up at a dreadful hour to see the sunrise, but in reality, it's those late-night genes that make you what you are.

PEER PRESSURE:
Wus or Winner?

You've been in sticky situations. Sometimes you stood tall and sometimes you folded. Take this easy quiz to discover if you're a wet noodle or a firm statue.

1. **You are at a strictly A-list party, and everyone (including your crush) is smoking pot. When it is offered to you, do you:**
   A inhale and enjoy. He'll love you now.
   B pass it on. You've got a cold.
   C pass it right along. It is not your thing.

2. **Your pals are going to shoplift some major stuff. When they ask to use your backpack to stash the "new wardrobe" in, do you:**
   A say, "Sure, just remember to zip it up."
   B say, "Okay, but just this time."
   C refuse. It's wrong and illegal.

3. **Last night your buds ditched your study session and went out. Now it's time to take the test. You're the only one who has studied and they want to cheat off you. You:**
   A say okay, but only if they promise to study a lot next time.
   B agree to, as long as they get you something good at the mall to compensate.
   C refuse. It's their fault they didn't study, and besides, cheating is wrong.

4. **Your dad just bought you a new car and lately you've become the taxi driver. Now you're sick of shuffling your friends around. Do you:**

- A do it anyway. They're your friends.
- B ask them to chip in for gas.
- C let them know that they are relying on you too much. It's time they took a turn.

5. **Your teammates want to cut down the soccer nets at a neighboring rival high school. You:**

- A volunteer to drive.
- B supply the scissors.
- C suggest another way to get under the other team's skin. For example, you could practice more so that you kick their butt in the next game.

Your Score

Mostly As: Wus. Start sticking up for yourself. Smoking pot shouldn't make a crush like you, and if it does, douse the flames on that romance fast! And if you don't want to do something, don't do it.

Mostly Bs: Somewhat Firm. Although you stand up for yourself once in a while, you need to hold your ground more often. Don't try to please others, especially if it means participating in risky activities like vandalism or shoplifting.

Mostly Cs: Stand-up Queen. Good for you! You hold your own when it comes to those dreaded positions. People will respect your decisions. If they don't, they aren't worth your time anyway.

are you **in love** ?
with yourself

Does the mirror have two faces, both yours? Are you your own best friend? Try your self-love profile to see if maybe you could be too far gone on yourself. Check true or false if any of these rings a bell.

1. At a sleepover, do you wear skimpy clothes to show off your bod, then criticize everyone else's?

True ___ False ___

2. If one of your buds buys the same shirt as you have, do you immediately think she's imitating you and get into a snit?

True ___ False ___

3. When you go out to dinner with a friend and her 'rents, do you pig out and order everything you want regardless of what it costs someone else?

True ___ False ___

4. Do you constantly make fun of your bud's other friends, then subject her to hours of talk on how great your other friends are?

True ___ False ___

5. While you are on the phone at a friend's house, you hear a piece of juicy gossip. After you hang up, your friend wants to know what you are laughing about. Do you brush her off, even though everybody else already knows?

True ___   False ___

6. Do you borrow your buds' clothes without asking, thinking that they will look better on you anyway?

True ___   False ___

7. When sleeping over at a bud's, do you automatically finish off the last ice pop without telling anyone?

True ___   False ___

8. When you and your bud pass a group of hotties, do you always comment that the guys are checking you out?

True ___   False ___

9. When your favorite song comes on the radio, do you make everybody else shut up, but then talk through all their faves?

True ___   False ___

10. Do you call your buds at three o'clock in the morning (knowing you're waking them up) because you want someone to talk to?

True ___   False ___

11. When you go to a party, do you think that the guests are lucky that you showed up?

True ___ False ___

12. If you and your buds goof up and get busted by her 'rents, do you accept your share of the blame?

True ___ False ___

Your Score

Mostly False: You're considerate, caring, and sharing. You're not at all conceited, and you probably have a lot of true friends.

Mixed True and False: You're somewhat inconsistent. Maybe as you grow up, you'll see it's important not to be self-centered.

Mostly True: Girl, you got it bad! For yourself! Shape up fast or your buds will outgrow you, leaving you to wonder why you're so lonely.

ACADEMY AWARDS:
Do You Pretend to Be Someone Else?

Scared to be yourself? Afraid people won't like you if you're not a weenie? Sure, there are times we all dive behind masks, but if you find yourself slipping into a role too often, maybe you should realize how rockin' you really are. Scope out our actors' audition to learn if you're starring in your own life or someone else's. Choose one column or the other.

	Real Me	Up for the Role
Your new crush is into soccer, so you try out for the team even though you're overscheduled.		
Your friends have all bleached their hair, so you lighten up, too.		
Your 'rents love you to be their "little girl" when their friends visit. Do you put on that super geeky dress?		

	Real Me	Up for the Role
You did so well in bio your teach wants you to go to science camp this summer. You're not interested. Do you go anyway?		
Your buds tease you about being so smart, so the next time you don't study and blow the big math test.		
You love to baby-sit, so Mom signed you up at a summer day camp with hordes of five-year-olds. Do you pretend it's great or tell her no thanks?		
Your older sister was a track star, but you really dig softball. Do you follow in her footsteps or do what *you* want to do?		
Your bud lends you clothing so you have can have a new look, but you're not really comfortable in it. Surprise! You're flooded with compliments. Do you head for the mall or go back to your old style?		

	Real Me	Up for the Role
Your dad surprises you with a new Jeep! You've always wanted a classic punch buggy. Do you peel out . . . or real out?		

SCORING

Mostly "Up for the Role": Step back and take a look—this is *soooo* someone else's life. Do you really like soccer? Are those clothes you? Who you are is important, too. Try to please yourself—you're worth it.

Mostly "Real Me": Bravo! You know who you are. What's even better, you know you don't have to be a chameleon to get people to like you. Good for you for not always following in others' footsteps.

are manners
for morons?

Manners are important for everyone! They're not just for adults or when you're trying to impress your crush's parents. Good manners are different from knowing which fork to pick up or how to order in a fancy restaurant. They're more about courtesy and kindness. Even Eeyore, Christopher Robin's favorite donkey, knows a little thought, a little consideration makes all the difference. How do your manners stack up? Are you polished, a diamond in the rough, or a dud spud?

When you telephone your bud's home, do you say:
- ❑ a) "Hi, this is Desiree. May I speak to Brian?"
- ❑ b) "Brian there?"
- ❑ c) "Yo, Bri."

There's a long line at the movie candy counter. You spot a bud. Do you:
- ❑ a) Cut in line by your friend, ignoring everyone else?
- ❑ b) Complain loudly about the slow-moving line?
- ❑ c) Take your place at the end of the line and catch up with your bud inside?

Company is arriving for dinner. Your parents are late. Do you:

- ❑ a) Answer the doorbell and chat pleasantly with the guests?
- ❑ b) Ignore the doorbell by playing loud music till the 'rents get home?
- ❑ c) Show the guests in but immediately get on the phone.

It's your birthday and your best friend gave you a present that totally sucks. You can't believe it! Do you:

- ❑ a) Vow to get even on her birthday?
- ❑ b) Pretend to vomit?
- ❑ c) Smile and say, "It's just great," hoping for better next year?

It's holiday time, and you always receive something in the mail from your aunt. You're so busy with your parties and buds that a thank-you note seems like a lot of work. Is it best to:

- ❑ a) Sit down right away and pen a friendly letter?
- ❑ b) Decide to telephone her when you get a chance?
- ❑ c) Blow her off because she doesn't have e-mail?

Dinner is over, and you're swamped with home-work. Do you:

- ❑ a) Bolt from the table?
- ❑ b) Ask to be excused, promising to help out more after exams?
- ❑ c) Give the dog your plate?

Your bud accidentally burps. What is your reaction?

❑ a) Laugh and call her a pig.

❑ b) Say, "Nice one, but I can do better," and burp loudly?

❑ c) Carry on as though nothing happened.

Your mom's friends are visiting with their annoying nine-year-old son. You:

❑ a) Swallow hard and entertain the kid as best you can.

❑ b) Pretend not to hear anything he says.

❑ c) Make fun of him and ask why he has no friends.

On a family vacation, you're suddenly joined by a flaky guest. You:

❑ a) Goof on him every chance you get.

❑ b) Drop strong hints about departing times.

❑ c) Let him tag along and just have fun.

Your best bud's family took you on vacation. Even though you didn't have the greatest time, do you:

❑ a) Thank them warmly and later drop a nice note?

❑ b) Tell your bud to say good-bye for you?

❑ c) Mutter thanks as you're running out?

You're stretched out on the family room sofa watching television when a new neighbor drops by. Your mom introduces you. Do you:

❑ a) Stand up and greet her politely?

❑ b) Mutter hello?

❑ c) Grunt, then continue watching your show?

You're invited for dinner at your best bud's house, but unfortunately you're running over an hour late. You:

❑ a) Relax, it's only your best bud's house.

❑ b) Get there as soon as possible.

❑ c) Call them immediately, apologizing for any inconvenience, and say you hope they have started without you.

You're watching a great movie when you leave the room to take a call. When you get back, your sneaky brother has switched the TV to a boring wrestling match. How do you get your tape back on?

❑ a) Telling him only airheads watch wrestling.

❑ b) Pointing out you were watching a tape and asking nicely if you could put it back on.

❑ c) Hide the remote control.

Your mom is single and she wants you to go to a party at the draggy neighbors with her. To get some mileage out of it, you:

❑ a) Argue and complain for at least two days.

❑ b) Point out that she will owe you big-time.

❑ c) Swallow hard and go graciously—after all, she does lots for you.

Today is your fave teach's fortieth birthday. To do something special for her, you:

❑ a) Make an announcement over the PA system informing everyone of her age.

❑ b) Bake her a cake with a big "40" on it.

❑ c) Throw her a surprise party after class, not mentioning her age unless she brings it up.

16 It's the night before your cousin's wedding and your house is packed with overnight guests. Dad asks you to go easy on the hot water. You love long, long, long showers in the A.M., so you:

❑ a) Cut back to ten minutes.

❑ b) Take your long shower at night.

❑ c) "Forget" and shower your regular time. After all, it's your house!

17 Mom expects you to set the table for dinner. You forget the napkins, knives, and half the glasses. When she busts you on it, you:

❑ a) Tell her something is burning on the stove.

❑ b) Complain that you have a lot of homework and storm out.

❑ c) Go and get the missing things.

Your Score

	Best	**So-so**	**Need Work!**
1.	a	b	c
2.	c	b	a
3.	a	c	b
4.	c	a	b
5.	a	b	c
6.	b	a	c
7.	c	a	b
8.	a	b	c
9.	c	b	a
10.	a	c	b
11.	a	b	c
12.	c	b	a
13.	b	a	c
14.	c	b	a
15.	c	b	a
16.	a	b	c
17.	c	a	b

are you a **party** pooper or a **party** person?

Party on or pass out? What's the scope on your partying style? Are you the life of the party or a killjoy? Check which one most describes you, true or false.

1. The homecoming dance is Saturday. You feel a cold coming on.
❏ **TRUE** ❏ **FALSE**

2. It's your best friend's birthday. Instead of partying, you'd rather take her out on your own.
❏ **TRUE** ❏ **FALSE**

3. Your bud drops by with a pizza and wants the rest of the gang to come over. You kick back and have fun.
❏ **TRUE** ❏ **FALSE**

4. For your Sweet Sixteen, Mom and Dad want to throw a big bash. You'd rather get a new VCR.
❏ **TRUE** ❏ **FALSE**

5. Your curfew is midnight, but you bail out of parties by ten.
❏ **TRUE** ❏ **FALSE**

6. When the Sunday paper arrives, you dive for the weekly TV section so you can plan for Saturday night.
❏ **TRUE** ❏ **FALSE**

7. You're uncomfortable at parties where you don't know everybody.

❏ TRUE ❏ FALSE

8. If you're invited to a costume party, you get dressed up in a cool outfit.

❏ TRUE ❏ FALSE

9. When the buds plan to party, you get in the swing of it by asking what you can bring.

❏ TRUE ❏ FALSE

10. You always want to arrive at parties as late as possible.

❏ TRUE ❏ FALSE

11. When you party, you have such a blast, you never want to leave.

❏ TRUE ❏ FALSE

12. If you're not doing something you love, you whine and mope.

❏ TRUE ❏ FALSE

13. The thought of an impromptu bash gets your juices going.

❏ TRUE ❏ FALSE

Scoring

	Party Person	Party Pooper		Party Person	Party Pooper
1.	false	true	8.	true	false
2.	false	true	9.	true	false
3.	true	false	10.	false	true
4.	false	true	11.	true	false
5.	false	true	12.	false	true
6.	false	true	13.	true	false
7.	false	true			

do you have way too much ATTITUDE?

You think you're cool, but do others? Do you routinely overreact to trivial situations? Do you think your whining is winning? Here's the scoop on having way too much of a bad thing. Circle the answer that has Way Too Much Attitude!

1. You're at a crowded restaurant and the service is way slow. To put the waiter in his place, you:

A. spill a glass of water.

B. ask him if there is a problem.

C. storm out in a huff.

2. On a family vacation, the hotel air conditioner breaks. You report it and hope it gets fixed soon. Meanwhile you're all sweltering. What's not cool:

A. going out and hoping to catch a breeze.

B. taking an extra-long cold shower while everyone else sweats.

C. calling the switchboard to complain every ten minutes.

127

3. At the movies, the couple in front of you won't stop talking. To shut them up you:

A. kick their seats.

B. snarl, "Cool it!"

C. ask them politely to be quiet.

4. You waited all night for tickets to a hot concert. Right before the box office opens, a bunch of jerks jump the line. To get them to back off you:

A. point out there is a line.

B. complain to everyone around you.

C. egg on your boyfriend to fight them.

5. It's prom night, and what a bummer! Becky is wearing the same special gown as you. How do you react?

A. Blow it off.

B. Remark loudly that the dress would look better if she were ten pounds thinner.

C. Refuse to go near her.

6. You're driving down a country road and the car in front of you is going twenty miles an hour. How do you get it to speed up:

A. lean on the horn.

B. flash your lights.

C. get your friends to moon it while passing.

7. **At the school carnival, a bud spills her pizza all over you. What do you do?**

A. Chew her out loudly.

B. Insist she switch clothes with you.

C. Finesse it by acting as though it's a minor inconvenience.

8. **You campaigned like crazy for class treasurer, but your nemesis Miss Priss won instead. What's your reaction?**

A. a pat on the back for the winner and thumbs up for everybody who helped her.

B. storming out of school before the announcements are over, screeching, "I've been robbed!"

C. asking everybody if they voted for your opponent.

9. **As always, you're running late for class. A bud walks by and says hi. You:**

A. snap, "I'm late!" and keep running.

B. say, "Wow! I'm *soooo* late! Catch you later."

C. scream, "Get out of my way!"

10. **It's the school's annual food drive and you volunteer to deliver fliers. One homeowner objects to your cause, so you:**

A. blow him off loudly as being cheap.

B. keep on delivering the fliers. After all, you're committed.

C. give up right there. If people don't appreciate you, why bother?

11. You're on the yearbook committee. Naturally you think photos of yourself are the best. What do you do?

Ⓐ Try to be fair by holding back on your ego trip.

Ⓑ Ask a bud on the committee to put in lots of you.

Ⓒ Stick all yours in anyway. That's why you're on the committee.

12. Your bud's mom took you on a dream vacation. To thank her for her generosity, you:

Ⓐ do nothing. After all you made it fun!

Ⓑ buy her a small memento.

Ⓒ point out all the other great vacations you had.

Scoring

1.	A-3,	B-1,	C-2
2.	A-1,	B-2,	C-3
3.	A-3,	B-2,	C-1
4.	A-1,	B-2,	C-3
5.	A-1,	B-3,	C-2
6.	A-2,	B-1,	C-3
7.	A-3,	B-2,	C-1
8.	A-1,	B-3,	C-2
9.	A-2,	B-1,	C-3
10.	A-3,	B-3,	C-2
11.	A-1,	B-2,	C-3
12.	A-2,	B-1,	C-3

Your Score

10 to 14 points: The Coping 'Tude. You bounce back from tricky situations faster than a rubber ball. You're secure and generous—and know how to turn a potential disaster into a face-saving plus. With skills like these, you'll go far.

15 to 20 points: Loony 'Tudes. You're not going to make too many friends by being rude or overly assertive. Take your down attitude and make it more up by learning how to roll more graciously with life's little punches.

20 to 30 points: Major Killjoy. It's a good thing you're a teen, because attitudes like yours will not fly in the competitive adult world. You need a major 'tude-up, then you'll be pulling in the hotties and the buds.

are you a
hypochondriac?

If Band-Aids and Ace bandages are your favorite acces-sories and you think doctors are fun to talk to, may we suggest a painless cure? Prop up your feet, take out a pencil (without jabbing yourself!), and fill out our hypo-chondriac test.

1. How many sick days (from school) do you swing a year?

A one to two.

B four or more.

C I'm too tired to think about it.

2. Whose number is first on your automatic dial?

A best bud.

B Chinese delivery.

C my pediatrician.

3. What section are you most familiar with in the drugstore?

A cosmetics and magazines.

B candy.

C cold and flu medications.

4. Your favorite television show is:

A Cher infomercials.

B *Late Night with Conan O'Brien.*

C *ER.*

5. Which is more painful?

A watching *Face the Nation.*

B trig finals.

C ingrown toenails.

6. Is there one tissue you prefer over others?

A They're all the same to me.

B Tissue? I don't even know you!

C The large-size ones medicated especially for colds.

7. When you get a new prescription, how do you feel about reading the entire label?

A burdened.

B read the label?

C excited.

8. When are you most likely to come down with the sniffles?

A after being with germy kids.

B the last day of school vacation.

C at any time.

9. What color would you like to paint your room?

A I just painted it to match my favorite nail polish.

B whatever Mom likes.

C hospital white.

10. In general, how often do you change Band-Aids?

A when they look dirty.

B when they fall off.

C every three hours.

11. How many different-sized rolls of gauze bandage do you own?

A one.

B the one I used for Halloween.

C every available size.

12. When you see a red splotch on your skin, what do you want Mom to do?

A Look at it.

B Write me a note to get out of gym.

C Examine it, discuss it, relate it to other splotches, call the dermatologist. Then inquire about it every half hour.

13. How familiar are you with the nurse's office?

A vaguely.

B nurse's office?

C semi-professionally.

14. What do you think of the expression "Time heals all wounds" ?

A It's probably true.

B It sounds good.

C I'm sure a person would need an antibiotic as well.

15. If you had to have medical treatment on your own, would you be able to recall the proper names of the prescriptions you've taken?

A If I hadn't taken too many.

B Prescriptions?

C Absolutely, with dates, dosage, and prescribing physician.

Your Score

Mostly As: Clean Bill of Mental Health. Sounds like you're sane about your body and able to function quite well in case of a mishap. Your priorities seem healthy.

Mostly Bs: Not Ambulance Squad Material. You're so laid-back, it's almost refreshing. Try to learn about CPR or first aid so you could help out in a real emergency.

Mostly Cs: Heal Thyself. You're overdosing on things! Unless you're pre-med, you seem a tad obsessed with things medical. Think about joining more clubs and getting out with your buds.

TEACHERS AND ATTITUDES

What's Happening in School

Teens spend more time in school than at home. Why? For one thing, it's the law! For another, it's so much fun. Yes, there's lots of work—tests, finals, SATs ('rents, are you listening?)—but there are also mega ways to have a blast. Are you doing the most for yourself? Are you giving and getting enough out of these years?

Take a moment between classes (your crush shrine can wait) and test yourself on your school cool. Remember, you're the teach, so give yourself all the bonus points you want.

making the **most** of **school**

You like your school and think you're doing well. But are you maxing the opportunities of these "golden years"? Sure, you like sports, but are you too lazy to go out for the team? Or what about that great school library that you've been in twice? (And that was to track down a friend to find out gossip!) There's so much out there to do for somebody who knows how to take it on. Review this test to see if you're open to new ideas and challenges.

1. **When you get assigned a huge term paper, you start working on it:**
   a. a week before it's due.
   b. right away. You really want to do well.
   c. halfway through the assignment period.

2. **You dig soccer, but your school unfortunately doesn't offer it. You:**
   a. decide to throw in the towel. You are too bummed.
   b. start your own intramural team.
   c. decide to play another sport.

3. **You want to help out with the homecoming float, so to pitch in you:**
   a. chip in five dollars for supplies.
   b. volunteer your driveway as the building site and organize a committee.
   c. paint the float but refuse to dress up for the big parade.

4. **Your school just put in a new computer system. You know that it will help your grades a lot, but when they offer a how-to session you:**
   a. bag it. You'll figure it out sometime.
   b. sign up. It'll pay off.
   c. sign up, but only if your friends come along, too.

5. **Out of the thirty clubs that your school has, you are a part of:**
   a. one. It looks good on your record.
   b. eight. You love being involved.
   c. two. It is all you have time for.

6. **The Guidance Department asks for volunteers for the community cleanup. You:**
   a. blow them off—cleaning is *not* your thing!
   b. sign up to see what it's like—and maybe meet some cute guys!
   c. promise yourself that you'll think about it.

7. **The girls' basketball team is in the state semifinals. The next game is away. Do you:**
   a. figure if they win, you'll hear about it.
   b. get up a group of buds and show up to cheer.
   c. plan to go to the next home game if they win.

8. The school walkathon is approaching and they need to raise a lot of money. You:

a. think about saving your strength for PE.
b. round up as many sponsors as you can.
c. sponsor another walker. Maybe you'll participate next year.

Scoring

Mostly As: Super Slacker. Get up and take part in your school. If you don't dig sports, join the debate club or try out for the play. Join the art club or practice Spanish after school. Once you find your niche, you'll have a great time.

Mostly Bs: Go-getter. Good for you for joining a couple of clubs and going to that help session for the new system in the library. It's great to be involved in your school. Your extra effort will pay off in the long run.

Mostly Cs: Halfway Player. It's good that you don't head home every day on the bus. But just hanging around school isn't great. Go to the yearbook meeting or join the photo club. Maybe basketball is your thing. Whatever! Start getting involved in your school. You'll meet new people and have a fantastic time.

What's the Right School Attitude?

Sure, you're bummed that you failed that test, but you can't throw a fit with the teach. So, you may have missed the goal in your soccer game, but you didn't have to yell at your teammate for making the bad pass. Do you have the right attitude for success in school? Check true for the situations that apply to you, and false for the ones that don't.

1. You're elected class president. Now that it's time to do the work, you aren't sure if you really wanted this job.

❑ **TRUE**
❑ **FALSE**

2. As captain of the school softball team, you organized a team bonding session at your house.

❑ **TRUE**
❑ **FALSE**

3. You just got assigned to groups for an oral presentation in French class. You flip through the script trying to find the smallest part.

❑ **TRUE**
❑ **FALSE**

4. In an attempt to get an A, you studied during lunch period. Then when you got a C, you were totally bummed.

❑ **TRUE**
❑ **FALSE**

5. When you are voting in the yearbook committee, you don't vote for Donna because she flirts with your boyfriend.

❑ **TRUE**
❑ **FALSE**

6. Your teacher offers help sessions for the final examination before school at the horrid hour of seven A.M. Even though you hate getting up early, you go anyway for the practice.

❑ **TRUE**
❑ **FALSE**

7. When the time comes to sign up for clubs, you join as many as you can.

❑ **TRUE**
❑ **FALSE**

8. You did lots of extra work in art class. Even though you didn't win the prize for best artist, you figure you'll still take art next semester because you love it.

❑ **TRUE**
❑ **FALSE**

9. You had the lead in last year's school play. This time you got a minor role. Even though you're disappointed, you'll still give it your all.

❑ **TRUE**
❑ **FALSE**

10. Billy needs extra help in math. Even though you're not crushing on him, you offer to tutor him after lunch.

❑ **TRUE**
❑ **FALSE**

Your Score

True on 1, 2, 3, 4, 5:
You need to shape up your attitude in school.
So what if Donna flirts with your boyfriend? Although her come-ons may cause tension, if she's the best one up for the office, then she deserves it. Also, one lunch period of studying doesn't justify any harsh feelings when you didn't ace the test. Try being a little more positive with your thinking. That'll help your perspective on things a lot.

True on 6, 7, 8, 9, and 10:
You have a school-smart attitude. Good for you for signing up for clubs. Bonus points for you for getting up early to go to the study session; it'll pay off in the end. Keep it up!

Is Your Teacher
Hassling You?

You're working your hardest, but you can't seem to live up to your teacher's standards. It's getting harder and harder to ace this class. You're constantly being picked on, and you're sick of it. Check out this quiz to find out if it's time to act. After reading all the scenarios, circle the ones that may apply to you.

1 You worked your butt off on your final paper. You and your buds thought it was the best paper in the class, but you got a mediocre C.

2 When it's time to be assigned to groups, this teacher always sticks you with the obvious slackers.

3 You are always picked to go first when giving presentations.

4 Although you participate in class discussions and do your part, the teacher's comments on your report cards are always lukewarm.

5 Your teacher constantly criticizes your work.

6 Other kids in the class comment on how the teacher hassles you.

7 You think you're always assigned the hardest topics for long reports.

8 Even though you score in the nineties on all your tests and pop quizzes, your teacher is always surprised by your high grades.

9 The teacher never mentions you by name when praising all the hard workers.

10 She always stands over you, eye-balling your tests and homework.

Your Score

If you circled:

One answer: Think about it. Maybe you are just overreacting. You're probably just bummed because you didn't do as well as you had hoped. Keep doing your part, and you'll be fine.

Two or three answers: Talk to your parents. Suggest a meeting at school. You are most likely correct in your assumptions about being treated unfairly. If this continues, you'll have to meet with your teacher soon.

Four and above: Time for a talk. First, tell your teacher how you are feeling and that your parents want you to meet. If the hostility continues, go to the principal with your parents. It needs to be stopped.

My Best Friend Cheats!
what should i do?

Teens are under lots of pressure in school: stiff competition, parent's expectations, teacher's expectations, their own self-image, college boards, entrance exams, and more. Sometimes they're way too busy with sports and extracurricular activities and the temptation to cheat becomes overwhelming. Do you know someone who's taking an unauthorized shortcut? See if you can read the signals and do the right thing.

1. **Your friend said she was up late with bad cramps and couldn't study for the math test. She wants to sit near you and copy. Should you:**

    A let her.

    B tell her it makes you uncomfortable.

    C inform the guidance department.

2. **Your friend already got one warning from the science teacher. Now she's moving her desk close to yours and shooting you pleading glances. Should you:**

    A write your answers large and if she reads them, so what?

    B carry on normally but talk to her after class so she won't compromise you again.

    C ask the teacher for a new seat.

147

3. **You wonder how your friend always aces the toughest exams without studying. On the way to class, a cheat sheet falls out of her binder. Do you:**

   A pick it up and give it to her in the hall.
   B leave it on the floor.
   C hand it over to the teacher before the test.

4. **Your bud started to hang with kids who brag about cheating and getting away with it. Her grades are soft and you're worried her new buds will be a bad influence. You:**

   A adopt a wait-and-see attitude.
   B share your concerns with her—in a gentle way.
   C call her parents.

5. **Your friend asks to copy your homework and the study hall monitor overhears and calls you both up to her desk. You:**

   A burst into tears.
   B point out that you didn't actually share the work and promise that it will never happen again.
   C tell the monitor that you weren't the one who asked—and ditch your friend to get out of it alone.

6. **During chemistry finals, you notice your bud's arm looks like she's just visited the tattoo parlor. Afterward, you:**

   A lend her your soap.
   B talk to her, suggesting ways you can study together to improve her grade.
   C tell everybody at lunch.

7. Your bud is so busy with student government that she doesn't finish her French paper. An upperclassman offers his from the previous year. Should you:

A turn a blind eye.

B persuade her to talk to the teacher about an extension.

C turn them both in, immediately.

8. Your buds tells you to get with it—everybody cheats. Do you:

A think that maybe she's right.

B explain that not only is her statement wrong, but it's also stupid, and that you can do well on your own.

C write a letter to the school newspaper denouncing the teachers' lax supervision.

9. Two kids are caught copying on a trig final and fail the course. One of them tells you your bud was cheating, too, but didn't get caught. Should you:

A keep quiet.

B tell her what was said about her.

C send an anonymous letter to her mother.

10. You found out that your friend cheated in pre-calc. You studied really hard and got a lower grade than she did. Now you feel resentful. You:

A congratulate her.

B tell her that cheating can destroy friendships, because it isn't fair to others.

C make her swear she'll never cheat again; otherwise you'll call her parents.

Your Score

There are no easy answers on this test because cheating is a real problem.

Mostly As: A Blind Eye. You're turning away from a tough situation. Are you hoping that if you ignore it, it will go away?

Mostly Cs: Hanging Judge. You're much too harsh! And *soooo* interested in punishment, rather than cure.

Mostly Bs: Care for You. You demonstrate that you're really concerned for your friend's welfare and for your friendship. You hope she'll change, but if she doesn't, you might have to rethink your commitment to her.

what does your locker say about you?

Next to a bedroom, a locker is a teen's most personal space. For anyone skilled at decoding nonverbal messages, lockers are a gold mine of information. Quiz yourself below to discover what your locker may be dishing about you.

1

I keep my locker locked with:
- ❑ a) heavy chain.
- ❑ b) office-issue combination lock.
- ❑ c) duct tape.

2

If you have a combo lock, how many people know the numbers?
- ❑ a) only myself.
- ❑ b) Mom, Dad, Grammy, the Guidance Department, the office staff, my personal diary, my stuffed bear, and me.
- ❑ c) I've lost count.

3

If your locker came to life as a dog, it would be:
- ❑ a) a pit bull.
- ❑ b) an adorable cocker spaniel with a plaid collar.
- ❑ c) a resourceful St. Bernard.

You celebrate holidays by decorating your locker with:

❏ a) mothballs.

❏ b) politically correct removable recyclable stickers.

❏ c) homemade cards from my buds.

Your crush shrine looks as though it could:

❏ a) fool your crush.

❏ b) please the office staff.

❏ c) join the homecoming parade as a float.

You would rather share a locker with:

❏ a) Johnny Depp.

❏ b) Michael J. Fox.

❏ c) Kramer.

What does your locker smell like?

❏ a) Lysol.

❏ b) Tic Tacs.

❏ c) cappuccino and socks.

If you could decorate your locker any way, it would be:

❏ a) the same as it is.

❏ b) stenciled in ivy and roses, with a smile button border.

❏ c) tie-dyed with a bulletin board for messages.

How long does it take you to locate your binders?

❏ a) I never lose them.

❏ b) no time at all! They're exactly where they belong!

❏ c) a semester.

If the school principal handed you a dream locker, where would it be?

❑ a) by the front door.

❑ b) near the library.

❑ c) next to the boys' locker room.

If a hottie mistook your locker for his, what would you do?

❑ a) Call the school security guard on your cell phone.

❑ b) Point out his mistake in a nice way!

❑ c) Introduce yourself.

On parents' night, you:

❑ a) say you're not authorized to open your locker.

❑ b) show Mommie and Pop-Pop your Laura Ashley coordinated book covers and things.

❑ c) tell the padres lockers haven't been assigned yet.

How many photographs of you are hanging up:

❑ a) none.

❑ b) one, in a small heart-shaped gold frame.

❑ c) zillions.

When hunks walk by as you're opening your locker, you:

❑ a) shield the interior by turning your back.

❑ b) wonder how they can wear such sloppy clothes.

❑ c) wave the door back and forth so they can get a whiff of your latest EDT.

What would you say about the size of your locker:

❑ a) It's adequate.

❑ b) Organizers and baskets work wonders in such small spaces!

❑ c) I'm looking for a locker mate who wants to share his locker so I can have more than one location.

Scoring

Mostly As: The X-Files. You don't want anybody messing with your space. Your locker is so off-limits it's practically classified. We hope you're not sending out these vibes to people, too.

Mostly Bs: It's an Up Thing! You like everything cheerful and pretty. With your organizational skills and perky attitude, you could have a great future in the space program.

Mostly Cs: Locker to Me. Size is no restriction for a party person with a heart as big as yours. You take everything easy, but you're no fool—you kept the 'rents at bay, and that's always important.

CHAPTER SIX

HOME LIFE
Parents, Sibs, and Your Space

Sometimes being a teen is so challenging, you wish the 'rents would cut you more slack. For instance, why does your room have to be super clean? Just because you haven't put away your summer clothes (from third grade), that doesn't mean you're heading for sure ruin, just that you're very busy. And those sibs, why can't they understand that your television picks are way more interesting than theirs? Or that invading your room could prove as dangerous as walking across an abandoned minefield? If only they were as understanding as your buds!

What are your views about the way parents are behaving today? Try taking the "Twenty-five Surefire Ways to Please or Peeve the 'Rents" quiz along with these others to discover how to make your home life as cozy and mellow as it should be.

25 Surefire Ways
to Please or Peeve the 'Rents

It always pays to keep parents happy! The following quiz contains surefire ways to impress Mom and Dad—and to tick them off. Let's see how you rate on the Please or Peeve quiz.

1. Do you clean your room without the 'rents asking, making sure, of course, to leave the door open so they can spot your hard work?
❏ **YES**
❏ **NO**

2. Do you "forget" to walk the dog, but promise you'll do better in the future?
❏ **YES**
❏ **NO**

3. Your crush drops by and finishes off Dad's favorite ice cream. When Dad discovers this, do you tell him he could shed a few pounds?
❏ **YES**
❏ **NO**

4. On your mom's birthday, do you place a bouquet of flowers on her bedside table?
❏ **YES**
❏ **NO**

5. Sure, you promised to clean your room, but the buds want to go blading. Do you dump all your dirty duds in a heap in the laundry?

❑ **YES**
❑ **NO**

6. Do you wash the family wheels and even clean the inside?

❑ **YES**
❑ **NO**

7. Do you nail down your solo at the recital?

❑ **YES**
❑ **NO**

8. Right before the 'rents' guests arrive, do you appear covered with temporary tattoos?

❑ **YES**
❑ **NO**

9. When you accidentally spill nail polish on the sofa, do you tell the 'rents to chill, you'll clean it later?

❑ **YES**
❑ **NO**

10. Do you study hard for finals and ace them all?

❑ **YES**
❑ **NO**

11. You love the new car. Do you offer all your friends rides home before asking Mom?

❑ **YES**
❑ **NO**

12. Do you surprise the 'rents with breakfast in bed (and clean up the kitchen afterward)?

❑ **YES**
❑ **NO**

13. Oops, have you locked the keys in the car, with the spare at home?

❏ **YES**
❏ **NO**

14. Do you pick out a tape Dad would like and actually watch it with him?

❏ **YES**
❏ **NO**

15. On Sunday afternoon, do you visit Mom's favorite old aunt with her?

❏ **YES**
❏ **NO**

16. The padres' new friends are coming for dinner. Do you greet them warmly and chat with them?

❏ **YES**
❏ **NO**

17. Do you ditch the folks at a family party to talk on the phone with your buds?

❏ **YES**
❏ **NO**

18. You arrange to meet Dad at the mall. Are you two hours late because you find so many cool things?

❏ **YES**
❏ **NO**

19. Do you call in when you promise to and even sound chipper?

❏ **YES**
❏ **NO**

20. The new retainer from your orthodontist is a drag. Do you "lose" it?

❏ **YES**
❏ **NO**

21. Do you borrow Dad's golf clubs and leave them outside for a week?

❏ **YES**
❏ **NO**

22. Do you volunteer Mom to bake four dozen brownies for the Latin party, but forget to tell her until the night before?

❏ **YES**
❏ **NO**

23. Dad mentions that he's expecting an important call. Do you get him right away when it comes?

❏ **YES**
❏ **NO**

24. It's your brother's birthday. Do you bake him his favorite cake?

❏ **YES**
❏ **NO**

25. It's Halloween. Do you stay home part of the night to help give out candy?

❏ **YES**
❏ **NO**

SCORING
Sure Pleases: 1, 4, 6, 7, 10, 12, 14, 15, 16, 19, 23, 24, 25
Sure Peeves: 2, 3, 5, 8, 9, 11, 13, 17, 18, 20, 21, 22

are my parents
Heading for a Divorce?

You love your parents and they love each other, too, right? What if you've noticed a few negative vibes or some tension? Here's a short true or false quiz to help you spot the danger signals that can lead to a divorce.

1. Your family used to eat together every night, but now you're lucky if you share a meal once a week.

❏ **TRUE** ❏ **FALSE**

2. Your 'rents haven't spent a lot of time together, at least time when they aren't fighting.

❏ **TRUE** ❏ **FALSE**

3. They used to sleep in the same bed. Now one of them is hitting the sack on the sofa.

❏ **TRUE** ❏ **FALSE**

4. When speaking about each other to you, they refer to the other as "your father" or "your mother."

❏ **TRUE** ❏ **FALSE**

5. The phrase "No matter what happens, I still love you" occurs quite frequently lately.

❏ **TRUE** ❏ **FALSE**

6. One of them has become a health nut and joined a gym.

❏ **TRUE** ❏ **FALSE**

7. One of them is on the phone a lot, but never in front of the family.

❏ **TRUE** ❏ **FALSE**

8. Your parents rarely do things as a couple anymore and even vacation separately.

❏ **TRUE** ❏ **FALSE**

9. There's a general lack of interest in maintaining the house.

❏ **TRUE** ❏ **FALSE**

10. They don't take photographs of family occasions much anymore.

❏ **TRUE** ❏ **FALSE**

Your Score

Did you answer more than four of them true?
If so, then it's time to sit down with your parents and have a talk. Although it may seem difficult, it is for the best. That way you can get some clear-cut answers and it will answer a lot of your questions. Also, just remember, as corny as it seems, your parents do love you no matter what. If they divorce, it's not the end of the world. Remember, don't blame yourself. You didn't do anything wrong.

can you handle
your
new
steps?

Dealing with parents can be tough enough, but add some step-'rents and step-sibs and life gets extra hairy. Check out these situations to see if you can handle the ch-ch-ch-changes. Make your mark next to what's most "you."

I. Your mom hints that your new stepfather wants to be called Dad. You:

A cry.
B laugh.
C say you will when you feel comfortable.

2. Your new stepmom wants to attend your softball games. You say,

A "No way!"
B nothing—you pretend not to hear.
C "Sure, when I'm ready."

3. One minute your new stepsister from hell likes you, the next she's ratting on you. Should you:

A trash her room.
B refuse to talk to her.
C ride it out; she'll come around to like you for the good person you are.

4. Your stepdad thinks he's perfect and rags you all the time. How do you get him to chill?

A Run away from home.

B Stay in your room.

C Explain that Mom always took care of any necessary discipline and say you'd rather go back to that system for a while.

5. When you went to Dad's for a weekend, his new wife told you she needed your bedroom for an office. You feel left out. How do you deal with this?

A Throw her things in the hall.

B Refuse to visit anymore.

C Ask for your own space—at least a dresser or closet.

6. Mom's way involved with her new hubby. How do you get her to do things together?

A Run up big bills on her charge card.

B Stay at your bud's a lot.

C Tell her you miss her and suggest an activity you both enjoy.

7. Your new stepsister seems to call all the shots. What should you do to get your way sometimes?

A Keep a list of who gets what and put it on the refrigerator door.

B Hide her favorite things.

C Tell Mom you're planning an family outing and go ahead with it.

8. **You feel like a shuttle bus between Mom and Dad. What's worse, they never get it straight when you're coming and going. Should you:**

   A refuse to visit.
   B hide out when it's time to go.
   C explain to both of them your topsy-turvy schedule is making you crazy.

9. **Whenever your step-sib comes back from a visit to her dad, she's loaded down like a toy store. You never get all that great stuff. How do you not feel jealous?**

   A Insist Mom even it up.
   B Watch TV rather than have dinner.
   C Say you feel left out.

10. **Your stepdad is always bad-mouthing your real dad. How can you get him to lay off?**

    A Point out that he's no prize either.
    B Leave the room when he's talking to you.
    C Explain to him and Mom that he's making you uncomfortable.

Your Score

Mostly As: Whack Job. Let out some of that anger and communicate with your mom or dad. Things have changed, but that doesn't mean you're not loved anymore.

Mostly Bs: Passive Aggressive. You pretend nothing's wrong, but wind up doing hostile things. Open up; you deserve to air your problems. If your parents don't know what's bothering you, how can they help?

Mostly Cs: Well-Adjusted. You're accepting the new reality and dealing well with it. Being able to talk openly is a sign of maturity. Go, girl, you have turned this situation to your advantage.

Good At **Compromising?**

You think your parents are ultraconservative, especially when it comes to chores, curfews, and privileges. In turn, they think that you have it "too easy." Try this quiz to learn how good you are at meeting people halfway.

1. **Your parents want you home by nine, but you want to stay out at least until midnight. You :**

a. budge for ten-thirty. Hey, it's only an hour and a half more than they originally wanted!

b. say you'll be home by nine, but sneak in at eleven.

c. refuse to compromise and end up fuming and staying home.

2. **For your allowance, you want a hefty twenty dollars a week, but they'll only shell out ten. You:**

a. settle for ten. It's better than nothing.

b. insist on $20. You have to have those shoes you spotted at the mall.

c. negotiate for fifteen. You can get the shoes in two weeks.

3. Your little twerp of a brother demands a ride to his friend's house on the other side of town. You:

a. drive him. Mom will be happy.
b. charge him five bucks for gas.
c. refuse; you already had plans. He can ride his bike.

4. You really want Chinese food, but your boyfriend wants Italian. You decide to:

a. get Italian, but whine throughout the meal.
b. insist on Chinese; you had pizza and pasta last night.
c. get yours from Chinese takeout, then pick up his and eat together at home.

5. Your parents want you to baby-sit your little sister. But you already had big plans with your friends. You:

a. say fine, but your friends can come over and chill.
b. refuse; they should have asked earlier.
c. agree to sit but at twice what they pay the normal baby-sitter. Plus, your sister has to go to bed at eight instead of her usual ten.

Your Score

1. a-1, b-3, c-2   **4.** a-2, b-3, c-1
2. a-2, b-3, c-1   **5.** a-1, b-3, c-2
3. a-1, b-2, c-3

1 to 5 points: Expert at Compromising.

You are great at meeting the padres halfway. They'll appreciate your being understanding and give you more privileges because of it.

6 to 10 points: Cool at Compromising.

You'll pitch in once in a while, but refuse to cancel plans that you already had. Try helping out a little more. It is amazing what coming home on time will do for you. (For one thing it'll give your parents incentive to let you stay out longer!)

11 to 15 points: Stone-Face.

You need to put your share in. You're part of a family, and you have to drive your brother around once in a while or baby-sit your sister. If you do things for them, they'll do things for you.

What's Your Bedroom Neatness Style?

Sure, you have plenty of stuff in your room, but does it still look the way you want it to? Take this quiz to find out what your bedroom is saying about you.

I. On the walls in your bedroom you have:

A some photographs of you and your friends and two Tom Cruise posters.

B plain white painted walls.

C photographs, posters, newspapers, pictures people have made for you, and souvenirs from every vacation that you've ever taken.

2. The sheets on your bed are:

A flannel and a little wrinkled.

B blue and red perfectly pressed cotton sheets.

C on the floor. Your bed is so covered in clothing and magazines, there's no room for sheets.

3. When people sleep over at your house, they sleep:

A next to you. After all, your bed is pretty big.

B on the trundle bed that neatly pulls out from under your bed.

C in the living room with you. You can barely find room on the bed for yourself. How are you going to fit two or more people in it?

169

4. When it's time to get dressed in the morning you find your clothes:

A half hung up in your closet, half still in the laundry basket. You haven't had time to put them away.

B all folded and organized by color in your dresser.

C on the floor. It's hard to tell which are clean and which are dirty.

5. During an average day you are in your room:

A when with friends and when you are getting dressed.

B all the time; you like the peacefulness of being alone.

C never; you practically need a map to get around in there.

6. When your mother sees your room she usually:

A tells you that your clothes will get wrinkled if you don't put them away.

B says that you are neater than she is and should look for a job as a housekeeper.

C screams, then grounds you from the mall.

7. If you had to clean your room it would take:

A twenty minutes.

B no time at all—it's already spotless.

C hours, maybe days.

8. How are your dresser drawers organized?

A Each drawer has general categories.

B Every inch is accounted for, with compartments for socks, underwear, and pj's.

C Your room is like a compost heap, with various layers of really old stuff smoldering away in there.

9. If you had to describe your room as a weather system it would be:

  A balmy and breezy.
  B perfect weather day after day, like California.
  C Hurricane Teen!

10. When you return from clothes shopping at the mall, do you:

  A watch TV, then put your things away.
  B rush to your room to hang everything up.
  C leave the shopping bags until you need something to wear.

Your Score

Mostly As: Casual Chick. You like to be able to relax in your room. You don't mind a little mess sometimes and you like your buds to feel comfortable so they'll want to hang out.

Mostly Bs: Neat Freak. You are practically neurotic about your room. You feel that it is a reflection of you and you want to appear like a totally clean person. However, others may be put off by your compulsiveness.

Mostly Cs: Genuine Pork. Try putting a few hours aside this weekend and make friends with a vacuum and duster. Nobody likes a slob, plus it's hard to get around in this world if you're mega-disorganized. Ask a parent or friend to help you; everybody will probably be happy that you are trying to clean up your act.

HELPER OR HEIFER:
Are YOU Doing YOUR Share?

Okay, nobody likes a nag, but do the 'rents practically have to e-mail you to get you to help out? Reality check: Everybody has to pitch in and it's a drag for others to have to keep asking you to do things over and over.

Maybe you're not nag material. Maybe you're one of those great teens who can handle helping out. To see your Pitch-in Profile, check which is most often true about you in the appropriate column, "Me" or "Not Me."

	Me	Not Me
1. Do you specialize in making a mountain of garbage?		
2. Is your bedroom floor hidden from sight?		
3. Have the 'rents taken to referring to your room as the landfill?		
4. Do you pick up your dirty clothes and put them in the hamper?		
5. Even know where the hamper is?		
6. Do you know how to do the laundry?		

7. Do you do it?

8. Ever replace the toilet paper?

9. Lounge around all day in your pj's while others are cleaning up?

10. Put away the groceries?

11. Pitch in when company is expected?

12. Have you developed an allergy to dust due to the condition of your bedroom?

13. Do you rake the leaves and shovel snow?

14. Know *how* to rake leaves and shovel snow?

15. Walk the dog?

16. Bag up empties for recycling?

17. Clean up spills before you have to call in the stain-removal experts?

18. Help load up the car for vacations?

19. Do you cook dinner when the 'rents are late or stressed out?

	Me	Not Me
20. Vacuum up when the place needs it?		
21. Know where the vacuum is kept?		
22. Know how to replace a vacuum bag?		
23. Have you ever gone to the grocery store without being asked?		
24. Do you clean up if your buds trash the kitchen?		
25. Are you familiar with the supermarket layout?		
26. Would you know how to get dishes clean if the dishwasher broke?		
27. Have you ever cleaned the bathtub?		
28. Washed the car?		
29. Put away the hose?		
30. Do you plan to do your bio paper on molds and spores because of the proliferation of dirty dishes in your room?		
31. Have you ever taken out the garbage?		
32. Refilled the ice cube trays?		

	Me	Not Me

33. Can you be trusted to take clothes to the dry cleaners?

34. Pick them up?

35. Could you find the screwdriver?

36. Does the term spring cleaning mean anything to you?

Your Score

If you checked "Not Me" for 1, 2, 3, 9, 12, and 30 and "Me" for all the rest: **Teen Clean Queen.** Congratulations! You are mature and considerate. You know how to pull your weight and your cooperative attitude bodes well for the future—in addition to making your parents happy now!

If you checked mostly "Not Me" except for 1, 2, 3, 9, 12, and 30: **Hel-lo, Miss Piggy!** Life with you must be a walk on the wild side! Let's get real and morph from lazybones to bitchin' by pitching in. Surprise your parents by doing something cool without a big nag session—you'll be amazed how it pays off!

Ready for the
new addition?

The stork is coming, but are you okay with it? Read this to find out if it'll be a welcome addition—and to figure out ways to help and not get stressed in the process. Circle the answers that fit your opinion of life with the new arrival.

1

You plan on helping out with diapers.

2

You would like to plan a family hour for your family to relax and have some quality time together after the baby arrives.

3

You are thrilled by the thought of getting to help out around the house more.

4

You're bummed because there will be more meals for you to cook.

5

Sure, at first the baby will be cute, but after she or he wakes you up five times in one night, you will feel like strangling the little darling.

You'll feel left out because the 'rents will pay too much attention to the new baby.

6

The thought of having a little bro or sis is exciting.

7

You know you aren't going to be able to skip out on the weekends anymore.

8

You think that decorating the baby's room will be fun.

9

After you have been voted "baby-sitter" for the rest of your life, you will have to say good-bye to your social scene.

10

How did it turn out? If you circled 3, 4, 5, 6, 8, and 10, you probably aren't too excited about the new arrival. No matter how much you want to ring its little neck for waking you up, just remember three things: one, your mother did it for you; two, maybe your older siblings did, too; and three, you wake up, but your mom has to get up.

To make the stork's landing a little softer, discuss how the baby will bring changes, both positive and negative. Don't overlook how valuable it is to help around the house. It'll alleviate a lot of stress on the entire family and make your parents chill on you!

DO YOU pamper your pet TOO MUCH?

If Fido and Fluffy are taking over your life, maybe you should consider putting them on a shorter leash. Before things get too wild, take this short quiz to see who's the real head of the household (this is also a good quiz for your parents to take).

1. Your pet goes in the car with you:
- **A** only to the vet.
- **B** on vacations.
- **C** everywhere: supermarket, dry cleaners, etc.

2. Where does your pet sit in the car?
- **A** In his crate or on the backseat.
- **B** On the floor in front of the passenger seat.
- **C** On your lap.

3. Do you feed your pet:
- **A** lowfat pet food only.
- **B** pet food and the occasional treat.
- **C** the last bite of everything, including ice pops.

4. Your pet sleeps:
- **A** in the kitchen.
- **B** on the bedroom floor.
- **C** next to you, under the covers.

5. How many toys does your pet have:

A three.

B five.

C over thirty.

6. How does your pet react when you return home?

A Greets you happily.

B Follows you around for a few minutes.

C Barks or purrs frantically and won't leave you alone.

7. You are upstairs in your bedroom. Your pet is:

A downstairs playing with a toy.

B down the hall sleeping.

C right next to you.

8. You make up nicknames for your dog or cat:

A never.

B sometimes, after he does something silly.

C several times a day.

9. Your pet has how many collars?

A one.

B one for each season.

C different ones for holidays.

10. When does your pet receive presents?

A never.

B Christmas and birthday.

C Christmas, birthdays, his half birthday, your birthday.

11. When you want to give your pet a special treat, you reach for:

A all-natural biscuits.

B cheese.

C ice cream or chicken fajitas or deli turkey or cheesecake.

12. You find yourself telling boring pet stories to your friends:

A never.

B occasionally.

C they're not boring!

13. Your most recent photograph of your pet is:

A from last year.

B from his birthday.

C in the roll that's being developed.

14. What is your pet's favorite holiday?

A Arbor Day.

B Groundhog Day.

C his birthday.

15. How fluent in English is your pet?

A He understands most commands.

B He's well trained.

C English is his second language.

16. Where's your pet while you are doing your homework?

A checking out the food bowl.

B curled up next to you.

C on top of your book.

Your Score

Mostly As: You're the Boss! Seems as though in your home, the pet knows his place.

Mostly Bs: No Pet Peeves! Your pet life is well balanced.

Mostly Cs: Pet Power! Owner overboard! You're totally in love with your pet—and it's probably mutual.

do you **want to**
be a good sib **?**

If sometimes you look longlingly at only children and think, "Wow! Do they have it easy!" it's normal. Being a sib can be really hard work, even if your sib is cool. You've got to share the 'rents' affections, priorities, and money! Often, for every wonderful thing sibs do, there seems to be an equal measure of annoying things. But like all relationships, it's two-sided and being a good brother or sister now will pay off big later. See how sincere your sib spirit is by answering true or false.

1. I'll pitch in and do my sib's chores when it's crunch time for her.
T___ **F**___

2. If I borrow something I return it in good condition. **T**___ **F**___

3. I often accuse Mom or Dad of playing favorites.
T___ **F**___

4. At holiday time I add up the value of what each of us got, and if my sib got more, I complain.
T___ **F**___

5. When my sib does something great at school, I congratulate him.
T___ **F**___

6. I forget to pass along phone messages.
T___ F___

7. We always have fun hanging out together on family vacations.
T___ F___

8. If the 'rents are on the warpath, I sound a warning. T___ F___

9. I tell my sib she looks good when she's getting ready to go out.
T___ F___

10. I never let anyone trash my sib. T___ F___

11. I don't take my sib's stuff without asking.
T___ F___

12. Ratting on her to Mom and Dad is my hobby. T___ F___

13. When she goes on-line, I turn on the kitchen timer and make her get off the second it rings.
T___ F___

14. If somebody tells me something nice about my sib, I pass it along.
T___ F___

15. I try not to polish off the last of my sib's favorite foods.
T___ F___

16. If he uses all the hot water before I shower, I go ballistic.
T___ F___

17. When I'm really irked, I hide his favorite things. T___ F___

18. We always do something special together for the 'rents' birthdays.
T___ F___

19. We share shotgun in the car. T___ F___

20. On the holidays, we always dig doing the same silly traditions.
T___ F___

Your Score

1. True
2. True
3. False
4. False
5. True
6. False
7. True

8. True
9. True
10. True
11. True
12. False
13. False
14. True

15. True
16. False
17. False
18. True
19. True
20. True

15 to 20 correct: No Quibbling, Super Sibling! Life is sweeter when you treat your sib like a friend. Bonus points for placing a high premium on family loyalty and never letting anyone trash your sib.

10 to 14 correct: Sibling Success. On the whole, your sibling relationship rocks. Perhaps you want to make it super strong by thinking about the areas that could use improvement.

1 to 9 correct: Sibling Downside. Are you seeing only the dark side of siblinghood? If things are really bad, you can't be too happy at home. Try talking to an adult whom you respect so you can get the help you need.

CHAPTER SEVEN

HOT LOOKS
Fashion and Beauty

What are the hot looks and the beauty bummers? What are the must-haves and the must-avoids? What's your beauty style—are you a glam queen or natural beauty? And do you want to morph from one to another?

Test yourself to discover your real views on fashion, and learn what you can do to maximize pluses and hide flaws. Fashion and beauty are all about making you look good, not about turning into a version of somebody else. Break out of stale beauty grooves and get into fresh new ones so that you feel confident. To get the look that gets the crushes, read on....

am i a
FashionAddict?

There is nothing that you love more than getting a new outfit. But has it gone too far when your clothes spill out of your closet? Take this quiz to find out the level of addiction. Answer true or false to the following questions

1. You have the same sweater in two or more colors.
❑ **TRUE** ❑ **FALSE**

2. It takes you more than ten minutes to get dressed in the morning.
❑ **TRUE** ❑ **FALSE**

3. When you shop by mail you get a discount because you've spent so much money.
❑ **TRUE** ❑ **FALSE**

4. Within a few hours of receiving a gift certificate to the Gap you've spent the whole thing plus some extra money you're saving.
❑ **TRUE** ❑ **FALSE**

5. You buy a great dress that you love and worship for the next week. Then you get another dress and your old favorite ends up on the floor.

❑ **TRUE** ❑ **FALSE**

6. When you watch *Clueless* you realize that you have more clothes than Cher and Dionne combined.

❑ **TRUE** ❑ **FALSE**

7. When you go away for the weekend it takes two huge suitcases to accommodate all of your clothes.

❑ **TRUE** ❑ **FALSE**

8. Your shoe wardrobe is so big, you've bought the same style and color twice!

❑ **TRUE** ❑ **FALSE**

9. While shopping at the mall, you've fallen in love with both a super pair of earrings and a great shirt. You're faced with the question of which is more important—clothing or accessories? Who knows? You decide to blow your whole paycheck and buy them both.

❑ **TRUE** ❑ **FALSE**

10. You have to buy new hangers every week to keep up with your new purchases.

❑ **TRUE** ❑ **FALSE**

Your Score

True to 5 or more questions:

It is time to get your priorities in order. Clothing isn't the most important thing in the world. Maybe you should set yourself a monthly limit and keep to it.

True to 2 to 4 questions:

You care about the way the look. You might care a little too much, though. Try not to let yourself get hung up in the clothing trap.

True to fewer than 2 questions:

Give yourself a pat on the back. You know that the world doesn't revolve around what you are wearing.

who's your
CELEBRITY TWIN?

When you watch *90210*, do you think you're seeing double—'cause there on the tube are the looks that most of your school is sporting? What about you? Is there a celebrity whose style could be yours? Steamy Tiffany-Amber Theissen? Trendy Jennifer Aniston, girl-next-door Sandra Bullock, or rocker Courtney Love's morph from trash to cash? Check off the categories to discover which celeb most resembles you—or if you have a composite twin.

	Hair	Makeup	Body Language	Clothes	Jewelry	Sex Appeal
Tori Spelling						
Jenny McCarthy						
Drew Barrymore						
Julia Roberts						
Ricki Lake						
Rosie O'Donnell						

Hair   Makeup   Body Language   Clothes   Jewelry   Sex Appeal

Barbra Streisand

Claire Danes

Melissa Etheridge

Jessie Spano

Brandy

Cher Horowitz

Gwyneth Paltrow

Pamela Lee

Alanis Morissette

Jennifer Aniston

Spice Girls

Lisa Kudrow

Ellen DeGeneres

Heather Graham

Neve Campbell

Alicia Silverstone

Liv Tyler

Hair   Makeup   Body Language   Clothes   Jewelry   Sex Appeal

Roseanne

Renee Zellweger

Courteney Cox

Brooke Shields

Winona Ryder

Tyra Banks

Naomi Campbell

Jewel

Kate Moss

Ivanka Trump

Madonna

Gabrielle Reece

Cameron Diaz

Jodie Foster

Kate Winslet

Andie MacDowell

Janet Jackson

can clothes make you
Popular?

Fashion manufacturers want us to think all their latest creations are must-haves. When we look at fashion ads we see beautiful people having fun, but can clothes really make you popular? Take our survey to learn more about your attitudes—and whether or not you need an adjustment. Mark "True" or "Bogus."

1. Cool clothes get you invited to A-list parties.
❏ **TRUE**
❏ **BOGUS**

2. Teachers call on you more often when you're well dressed.
❏ **TRUE**
❏ **BOGUS**

3. It is better to be "Best Liked" than "Best Dressed" in the year-book.
❏ **TRUE**
❏ **BOGUS**

4. You need lots of new clothes in order to look good.
❏ **TRUE**
❏ **BOGUS**

5. Guys rarely notice if you wear the same thing twice in a week.
❏ **TRUE**
❏ **BOGUS**

6. Wearing clothes that are not the latest makes you a geek.
❏ **TRUE**
❏ **BOGUS**

7. It doesn't make you less of a person to have a small wardrobe.

❏ TRUE
❏ BOGUS

8. Lending your buds your new and expensive clothes will make them like you.

❏ TRUE
❏ BOGUS

9. It's important to tell everybody how much you pay for your clothes so they know what a great dresser you are.

❏ TRUE
❏ BOGUS

10. A smart dresser always buys two or three of the same thing as backup.

❏ TRUE
❏ BOGUS

11. The first thing you notice about a person is if she's wearing hot designer clothes or crummy clothes.

❏ TRUE
❏ BOGUS

12. Shoes are the biggest indicator of fashion savvy. You shouldn't be caught with anything but the latest.

❏ TRUE
❏ BOGUS

13. Style is more important than cost, and good grooming is more important than style.

❏ TRUE
❏ BOGUS

14. You should wait to see what the seniors wear before doing your school shopping.

❏ TRUE
❏ BOGUS

15. If somebody says you look nice, you automatically assume it's your clothes.
❏ TRUE
❏ BOGUS

16. You should buy way more clothes than you need just to be on the safe side.
❏ TRUE
❏ BOGUS

17. Only the best-dressed kids are elected to the student government.
❏ TRUE
❏ BOGUS

18. All the popular girls wear clothes that look as though they came off the runway.
❏ TRUE
❏ BOGUS

19. Mother Teresa made a larger contribution to the world than Calvin Klein.
❏ TRUE
❏ BOGUS

20. Good-looking sales-people in your favorite stores intimidate you.
❏ TRUE
❏ BOGUS

21. When you read fashion catalogs, you think you will be as beautiful as the models if you wear the same expensive clothes.
❏ TRUE
❏ BOGUS

22. You make fun of people in school because of their clothes.
❏ TRUE
❏ BOGUS

23. Interviews go better when you're confident about your appearance.
❏ TRUE
❏ BOGUS

24. If your clothes are clean and attractive, that should make you look good.
❏ TRUE
❏ BOGUS

25. When you're a teen, your style says something cool about you—not about the 'rents bank account.
❏ **TRUE**   ❏ **BOGUS**

Your Score

1. Bogus	8. Bogus	15. Bogus	22. Bogus
2. Bogus	9. Bogus	16. Bogus	23. True
3. True	10. Bogus	17. Bogus	24. True
4. Bogus	11. Bogus	18. Bogus	25. True
5. True	12. Bogus	19. True	
6. Bogus	13. True	20. Bogus	
7. True	14. Bogus	21. Bogus	

Mostly Correct: Looking Good! You've learned the right values about people and things—and don't easily get your head bent out of shape by others. Your attitude makes you popular with hotties and buds alike.

Mostly Incorrect: Yo! 'Tudegirl! You waste a lot of time worrying about what others think. You've got to put a more positive spin on things—like friends, sports, and school—and stop thinking about the life on the surface.

what'syourimage?

No single image fits everybody. Some of us want to be funky like the Spice Girls or squeaky clean like Ally McBeal. What defines your image? Check the box which best describes you:

1 Your favorite catalog is:
- ❑ a) Tiffany's
- ❑ b) J. Crew
- ❑ c) Victoria's Secret
- ❑ d) L. L. Bean
- ❑ e) Delia's

2 When you buy shoes, which store do you cruise for?
- ❑ a) Nordstrom
- ❑ b) The Athlete's Foot
- ❑ c) Nine West
- ❑ d) The thrift store
- ❑ e) Army-navy store

3 When shopping for makeup, you opt for:
- ❑ a) Clinique
- ❑ b) The drugstore
- ❑ c) Cosmetics Plus
- ❑ d) The health food store
- ❑ e) The party store

Which wardrobe rocks you the most?
- ❑ a) Kelly's on *90210*
- ❑ b) Anything on a Nike commercial
- ❑ c) The cast of *Cats*
- ❑ d) The Smith & Hawken catalog
- ❑ e) Kiss's

What's your favorite snack?
- ❑ a) Sushi and Perrier
- ❑ b) Pizza
- ❑ c) Salsa and chips
- ❑ d) Granola bars
- ❑ e) Candy

What television event do you really dig?
- ❑ a) The presidential elections
- ❑ b) The Olympics
- ❑ c) Miss America Pageant
- ❑ d) National Geographic specials
- ❑ e) The Grammys

If you could have any pet, it would be:
- ❑ a) A bichon frise
- ❑ b) A Labrador retriever
- ❑ c) A fluffy angora kitten
- ❑ d) Any pet from the animal shelter
- ❑ e) A troll

Your dream vacation is: 8

❑ a) Nantucket
❑ b) The Rockies
❑ c) Disney World
❑ d) The beach
❑ e) New York City

You think women should strive most for: 9

❑ a) Equal pay
❑ b) Prime-time sports
❑ c) Effective birth control
❑ d) Love, peace, and happiness
❑ e) Low-rate loans

What would you most like to get for Valentine's Day? 10

❑ a) Gold hoop earrings
❑ b) Tickets to a pro basketball game
❑ c) A lace bustier
❑ d) A candle-making kit
❑ e) A clean bill of health

Your Score

Mostly As: Preppie with Personality. You lean toward class and the classics: French perfumes, silk shirts, romantic trysts at a cappuccino bar.

Mostly Bs: Athletic Girl. You shine anywhere because you're so buff—long lovely walks along the beach or snuggled up in front of the fireplace with a beau and a book.

Mostly Cs: Party Girl. You love everything soft and feminine, and so enjoy being a girl! You're glamorous, flirty, and always on! Guys are probably standing on a conga line to get close to you.

Mostly Ds: Green Queen. You love everything natural and down to earth. Nothing artificial about you; you're pure and beautiful. Rainy fall nights or early morning dews find you at your most radiant.

Mostly Es: So Rockin'. Everything about you is turned on. You're a high-voltage person who likes to walk on the wild side. Music, videos, poetry, art—and tons of dazzled men folk—keep you company.

Turn-on . . . or Turnoff?

Sure, you love the natural look of your underarm hair, but does everyone else? And by the way, do you think those "funny" noises you make with your body are really amusing? Check out this quiz to learn whether you are turning people off or on by checking off what you think about each situation—is it a turn-on or turnoff?

1. You haven't replaced your stinky gym socks in months—they could run the mile by themselves!
❑ TURNOFF   ❑ TURN-ON

2. Sitting in front of you in chem class every day is the worst case of split ends on earth!
❑ TURNOFF   ❑ TURN-ON

3. You dig this yummy hunk except for one thing— he's a maestro at mouth farts.
❑ TURNOFF   ❑ TURN-ON

4. Right before the sleepover party, you do a quick pedicure so your feet look pretty.
❑ TURNOFF   ❑ TURN-ON

5. Hottie of the month is beeping his horn, and yipes! you haven't had time to shave your brier-patch legs. You go anyway.

❏ TURN**OFF**   ❏ TURN-**ON**

6. Mom's big office party is a must-show, so you make sure your teeth are sparkling clean and flossed.

❏ TURN**OFF**   ❏ TURN-**ON**

7. When someone holds open a door for you, you always say, "Thank You."

❏ TURN**OFF**   ❏ TURN-**ON**

8. It's prom night and you have to decide what nail polish would go with your white dress. How about two-inch falsies in dark green?

❏ TURN**OFF**   ❏ TURN-**ON**

9. When you're nervous, you pick at your face and hair.

❏ TURN**OFF**   ❏ TURN-**ON**

10. When you give your hottie a quick kiss in the school caf, you don't brand him with your lipstick.

❏ TURN**OFF**   ❏ TURN-**ON**

11. Lunchtime in your school cafeteria is like feeding time at the zoo—only worse, cause you're covered with food stains and smell bad all day.

❏ TURN**OFF**   ❏ TURN-**ON**

12. Why do some people always leave the toilet seat up? Is it a

❏ TURN**OFF**   ❏ TURN-**ON**

13. Eating and talking at the same time is a
❏ **TURNOFF**   ❏ **TURN-ON**

14. You try not to rub your eyes all day so you don't get raccoon eyes.
❏ **TURNOFF**   ❏ **TURN-ON**

15. How do you think Dad feels about the nose rings you wore to his office Christmas party?
❏ **TURNOFF**   ❏ **TURN-ON**

16. Early-morning English muffins at school are the best. You always make sure to wipe off any crumbs or butter from your mouth.
❏ **TURNOFF**   ❏ **TURN-ON**

17. You've just come in from running and you're dripping with sweat! Is it a ❏ **TURNOFF** or a ❏ **TURN-ON** to join someone who's eating?

18. Your nails are bitten to the quick.
❏ **TURNOFF**   ❏ **TURN-ON**

19. You listen as well as you speak.
❏ **TURNOFF**   ❏ **TURN-ON**

20. You're sleeping at your bud's. The next morning you show up at the breakfast table in your pj's.
❏ **TURNOFF**   ❏ **TURN-ON**

21. Whenever you have a case of the flakes, you haul out the dandruff shampoo.

❑ TURN**OFF**   ❑ TURN-**ON**

22. You and your buds borrow Mom's new car, then return it with coffee cups, soda bottles, and food wrappers all over the floor.

❑ TURN**OFF**   ❑ TURN-**ON**

23. You have a new lab partner—and he's *sooo* hot! You always make sure you smell yummy with a light, sexy EDT.

❑ TURN**OFF**   ❑ TURN-**ON**

24. You've got a bad cold and your nose won't stop running. You stock up on scented, medicated tissues so you won't give it to anybody else or make a spectacle of yourself.

❑ TURN**OFF**   ❑ TURN-**ON**

25. You fall on the track and scrape your knee. Before the next class, you make sure your wound is taken care of and looks clean.

❑ TURN**OFF**   ❑ TURN-**ON**

26. Your voice sometimes gets too loud when you're nervous or excited. That's why you try to control it as much as possible.

❑ TURN**OFF**   ❑ TURN-**ON**

Your Score

The TURNOFFS are 1, 2, 3, 5, 8, 9, 11, 12, 13, 15, 17, 18, 20, 22.

The TURN-ONS are 4, 6, 7, 10, 14, 16, 19, 21, 23, 24, 25, 26.

If you made the right call for most of the questions: Turned Way On! and nice manners. Keep this up and the guys will be falling at your well-groomed feet. Bonus points for listening a lot and saying thank you.

If you bombed: Turned Off. Girl, you need major help! First, cool it with the dirty duds. Then if you have any nervous habits, pay attention to them or ask a trusted bud to remind you to stop. By focusing, you'll soon blossom into the sweet-smelling flower you are.

are **you** *too* into **your** looks?

If the cosmetics counter has become your new address and all your spare cash is tied up in nail polish, maybe it's time to peel back some of those layers and see the real you. Put down the mirror for a few minutes and take this test.

1. What is the average number of bottles of shampoo and conditioner in your bath?

A Two dozen, plus whatever is new.

B Fewer than five of each.

C Two of each.

2. Have you ever seriously considered any of the following?

A Shaving your legs only when necessary.

B Buying every new razor on the market.

C Full-leg laser hair removal.

3. Is it possible for you to go to the drugstore without checking out the cosmetics?

A Sure, if I have no money.

B Only if Dad's with me.

C Why would I?

4. What is your favorite pastime?

Ⓐ Giving myself a manicure and pedicure.

Ⓑ Reading a novel.

Ⓒ Shopping at the mall.

5. Is it a bad day for you if:

Ⓐ You spill nail polish on your homework.

Ⓑ Your hair frizzes up.

Ⓒ You bomb on a big exam.

6. Who has the most natural look?

Ⓐ Tori Spelling.

Ⓑ Chelsea Clinton.

Ⓒ Elvira.

7. Your best bud gets a fabulous new hairstyle. You:

Ⓐ Run to the parlor immediately to copy it.

Ⓑ Tell her, "You look cool."

Ⓒ Wait till hers grows out before getting yours done the same way.

8. It takes you how long to get ready in front of the mirror?

Ⓐ One CD plus.

Ⓑ Twenty minutes or more.

Ⓒ Mere minutes: a lip gloss and hairbrush are good enough.

9. Who is your hero?

Ⓐ Jackie Joyner-Kersee.

Ⓑ Bobbi Brown.

Ⓒ Amanda Woodward.

10. If your buds throw an impromptu party, what's your first reaction:

Ⓐ How much time do I have to get ready?

Ⓑ I hope Cindy doesn't wear her new dress.

Ⓒ Will there be any great guys there?

11. Which would you read first in the newspaper?

Ⓐ Discount drugstore ads.

Ⓑ Television listings.

Ⓒ Current events.

12. Which would you rather do?

Ⓐ Shop.

Ⓑ Go to a musical.

Ⓒ Watch reruns of *The Brady Bunch*.

13. What's the best way to project healthy self-esteem?

Ⓐ wearing Calvin Klein perfume.

Ⓑ standing straight and smiling.

Ⓒ getting your hair done.

Your Score

1. A-3, B-2, C-1	8. A-3, B-2, C-1
2. A-1, B-2, C-3	9. A-1, B-2, C-3
3. A-1, B-2, C-3	10. A-3, B-2, C-1
4. A-3, B-1, C-2	11. A-3, B-2, C-1
5. A-2, B-3, C-1	12. A-3, B-1, C-2
6. A-2, B-1, C-3	13. A-2, B-1, C-3
7. A-3, B-1, C-2	

13 to 20 points: **Pretty Sane Lady.** You're into the real world and others, not just yourself. You know the way to look good is to feel good.

21 to 29 points: **Blind Spot.** Sometimes we can't see how self-devoted we are. Maybe it's time to see inside your head, not just focus on the outside.

30 to 39 points: **Makeup? Wake Up!** You've got a major case of Surface Fever. The cure: soap and water, and lots of healthy new activities.

Grunge to Glam—
Getting There

Ever since Cinderella stepped out of her glass coach and landed her crush, Prince Charming, we've been hooked on Befores and Afters. Remember Julia Roberts in *Pretty Woman* or Julia Ormond in *Sabrina*? Same plot. But have you ever noticed that before every Cinderella becomes a total babe, she needs help? Be your own fairy godmother and quiz yourself on ways to morph from grunge to glam. Match the "before" grunge look to the "after" glam.

Grunge

___1. Sneakers with holes in them
___2. Stained teeth
___3. Clothes covered with pet hair
___4. Dark makeup
___5. Butch boots
___6. Flannel shirts
___7. Smelly backpacks
___8. Stretched-out pants
___9. Black nail polish
___10. Ankle tattoos
___11. Body piercing
___12. Fluorescent hair
___13. Note binders smeared with ink

___14. Oversize T-shirts
___15. Chunky plastic rings
___16. Smell of tobacco
___17. Bad language
___18. Crotch-length skirts
___19. Colossal men's shirts
___20. Shaved heads
___21. Thigh-high boots
___22. Jeans with huge bum holes
___23. Head to toe leather
___24. The Armed Forces look
___25. Ripped jackets
___26. The druggie look

Glam

A. Chunky oxfords
B. Fleeces
C. Natural makeup
D. Healthy hair
E. Slit skirts
F. Self-esteem
G. T-strap sandals
H. French manicure
I. Anklets

J. Highlighted hair
K. Chenille Ts
L. Birthstone ring
M. Wit
N. A nice EDT
O. Khakis
P. Organizers
Q. Bright smile
R. Clean clothes

S. Fitted button-downs
T. The workout look
U. Running shoes
V. Crocheted bags
W. A healthy glow
X. The natural thing
Y. Quilted jackets
Z. Straight-leg jeans

Answers

1. A	8. O	15. L	22. Z
2. Q	9. H	16. N	23. X
3. R	10. I	17. M	24. T
4. C	11. F	18. E	25. Y
5. U	12. J	19. S	26. W
6. B	13. P	20. D	
7. V	14. K	21. G	

Beauty Q&A:
Myth or Magic?

Ever since the days of Cleopatra (remember her—Elizabeth Taylor?) people have been slaves to beauty. In fact, the Egyptians invented many cosmetics we still use today like eye shadow and kohl liner. To be a modern-day temptress, quiz yourself on these basics. First, answer these true/false questions.

1. Conditioners can repair broken hair.

❏ **TRUE** ❏ **FALSE**

2. Acne is caused by oily foods.

❏ **TRUE** ❏ **FALSE**

3. Cellulite cannot be eliminated with expensive creams.

❏ **TRUE** ❏ **FALSE**

4. Eye makeup should always be removed before sleeping.

❏ **TRUE** ❏ **FALSE**

5. Gelatin is good for your nails.

❏ **TRUE** ❏ **FALSE**

6. You don't have to wear sunblock on overcast days.

❏ **TRUE** ❏ **FALSE**

7. Expensive vitamins don't take the place of a nutritious diet.

❏ **TRUE** ❏ **FALSE**

Scoring

1. False. Despite manufacturers' claims, nothing repairs broken hair.

2. False. Acne is caused by pores being clogged by too much oil produced by the body, not from foods.

3. True. Cellulite can be controlled only by exercise—or by liposuction, which is costly, extreme, and should not be considered by teens.

4. True. Remove eye makeup with a gentle cleanser.

5. False. Nothing helps fragile nails but keeping them short and avoiding acetone nail polish remover.

6. False. Even on a cloudy day the sun's rays can still cause damage.

7. True. You can easily get all your vitamins from food if you eat a balanced diet.

Now, pick the right answer from the word list.

WORD LIST

Split ends	**Fifteen**	**Acetone**
Eight	**Eight**	**Mascara**
Static electricity	**Sunblock**	**Showering**
Lemon	**Smoking**	

1. How many glasses of water should you drink a day for clear skin? _____

2. Blow-drying wet hair causes what damage to it? _____

3. Spraying your hairbrush with hair spray will help control what problem?

_____

4. How many hours of sleep should you get at night? _____

5. If your hair is oily, try a rinse with what?

_____

6. What protects better than a sunscreen against harmful UVA and UVB rays? _____

7. What is the least SPF recommended for daily wear? _____

8. Which eye makeup should definitely be replaced at least three or four times a year?

_____

9. What can cause bad breath?

_____

10. Avoid dry nails by not using polish removers containing what?

_____

11. Deodorant is best applied after what?

_____

Answers

1. Eight
2. Split ends
3. Static electricity
4. Eight
5. Lemon
6. Sunblock

7. Fifteen
8. Mascara
9. Smoking
10. Acetone
11. Showering

how did
mother nature
treat you ?

Not even the most gorgeous models in the world totally dig their looks. There's always something less than perfect—short legs, deeply set eyes, small lips. The bad news is that you can't reinvent yourself; the good news is that you can diminish or conceal many problems with smart makeup, hairstyles, and clothes. See if you can find the solutions for these genetic bum-outs by circling the right answer.

1. Big chest, little hips. Wear:

- **A** baggy shirts
- **B** jump suits
- **C** tops that hug the body gently

2. What neckline works best on short necks?

- **A** turtleneck
- **B** scooped
- **C** crew

3. A low forehead can be improved with:

- **A** bangs
- **B** a side part
- **C** shaving

4. The best way to shape bushy eyebrows is with:

A tweezing, done at a good salon

B gel

C wax

5. Small, deep-set eyes can be enhanced with:

A more sleep

B geisha-girl white makeup

C well-shaped brows and concealer

6. Puffy eyes can be improved by:

A drinking eight glasses of water a day

B expensive creams

C sunglasses

7. Oily skin needs:

A matte, oil-free foundation

B heavy cover-up

C lots of tissues

8. What are the most flattering pants for heavy hips and thighs?

A bell-bottoms

B super baggies

C classic-cut jeans

9. Baby-fine locks can be controlled with:

A gobs of gel

B protein shampoos and conditioners

C heavy hair spray

10. To give contour to a round face:

   A Use a pretty blush to add color, then concentrate on your eye and lip makeup.

   B Have cheekbone implants.

   C Wear long straight hair.

11. Are your lips lopsided? Is the top thin and the bottom full? What to do?

   A Wear dark lipstick on the bottom, bright on top.

   B Outline just the top lip with a pencil then add lipstick to both lips.

   C Make your upper lip bigger by going outside the lip line.

12. Short, stubby fingers appear more delicate by:

   A lengthening exercises

   B lots of silver rings

   C manicures with shimmery colors close to your skin tone

13. Eyelashes that are on the skimpy side can be enhanced with:

   A false eyelashes

   B purple mascara

   C two coats of mascara (be sure they dry in between)

14. All your friends are runway tall. You're a shrimp. How can you gain in stature?

   A dress in the same color families

   B wear tall heels with everything

   C concentrate on vertical stripes and big hairdos.

15. How can you make large pores appear smaller?

A use a heavy cover-up

B apply plenty of eye makeup as a distraction

C use oil-free moisturizer and foundation

16. What's a great skirt to "stretch out" short legs?

A floor length

B mini

C flare

17. Banish dark under-eye circles with:

A extra-long bangs

B dramatic eye shadows

C concealer that matches your foundation, then a dusting of powder.

18. Enhance small breasts with:

A a thirty-pound weight gain

B miracle bras

C erect posture

19. Control frizzy hair with:

A a weed whacker

B expensive conditioners

C blow-drying hair with a large brush

20. Slim down heavy thighs with:

A liposuction

B exercise

C panty hose

Answers

1. C	6. A	11. B	16. B
2. B	7. A	12. C	17. C
3. B	8. C	13. C	18. C
4. A	9. B	14. A	19. C
5. C	10. A	15. C	20. B

WHAT'S YOUR
Beauty Style?

Who's the true you? On the left are basic beauty types and on the right attributes of each style. Let's see how sharp you are at matching them up. Draw a line from beauty types to the corresponding characteristics.

Beauty Types

OUTDOORSY

REGAL

CLASSIC

DELICATE

COOL

CHAMELEON

NATURAL

GLAMOROUS

SEXY

FUNKY

MOD

Characteristics

Light blush

White lips

Long, shiny hair

Light, soft makeup

Pale colors

Clear gloss lipstick

Super-straight hair

Blue eyes

Purple lipstick

Natural eyebrows

Courteney Cox

Hair with sun streaks

Beauty Types

OUTDOORSY

REGAL

CLASSIC

DELICATE

COOL

CHAMELEON

NATURAL

GLAMOROUS

SEXY

FUNKY

MOD

Characteristics

Bronze tan

Highlighted hair

Pastels

Kate Moss

Fine features

Bare feet

Page boys

Shades of plum

Crimped hair

Red mouth

Brooke Shields

Braids

Spiky eyelashes

Pale brows

Dark roots

Lemony fragrance

Velvet headbands

Hair swatches

Cornrows

Dark colors

Real jewelry

Paloma Picasso perfume

Answers

Outdoorsy: bronze tan, bare feet, hair with sun streaks

Regal: highlighted hair, real jewelry, velvet headbands

Classic: long, shiny hair, natural eyebrows, light blush

Delicate: pale colors, fine features, Kate Moss, light makeup

Cool: blue eyes, pageboys, pastels

Chameleon: Brooke Shields, braids, hair swatches

Natural: clear gloss lipstick, lemony fragrance

Glamorous: red mouth, crimped hair, cornrows

Sexy: shades of plum, Courteney Cox, Paloma Picasso perfume

Funky: dark roots, dark colors, purple lipstick

Mod: super-straight hair, spiky eyelashes, pale brows, white lips

Plastic Surgery:
Do You **Really** Need It?

Are you completely bummed out over a feature? Do you imagine parts of your body look as though they were designed by Walt Disney? Whether it's pancake breasts, big moles, or whatever, before you seriously nag the 'rents about surgery, you might want to ask yourself:

1. I avoid mirrors because I see only something I hate.

❏ **TRUE** ❏ **FALSE**

2. For the longest time, I've been so troubled by my looks that I don't like to dress up and go out.

❏ **TRUE** ❏ **FALSE**

3. All the rest of my features match except for this one horrible thing.

❏ **TRUE** ❏ **FALSE**

4. I don't like meeting new people because they stare at me.

❏ **TRUE** ❏ **FALSE**

5. No matter how much I diet, exercise, or use makeup, I can't get rid of my problem.

❏ **TRUE** ❏ **FALSE**

6. My best friend had a nose job. My nose is bigger than hers was. I need one, too.

❏ **TRUE** ❏ **FALSE**

7. I tried different noses on computer imaging. If I have a nose job, I should pick the one I like, not my bud's favorite.

❏ **TRUE** ❏ **FALSE**

8. Celebrities always look better in their after photos. I should have surgery, too.

❏ **TRUE** ❏ **FALSE**

9. My brother and his friends call me Dumbo. I don't think my ears are large, but if it shuts them up, I should go for surgery.

❏ **TRUE** ❏ **FALSE**

10. At the beach, the girls who get the hot looks all wear bikinis. I should get a tummy tuck.

❏ **TRUE** ❏ **FALSE**

Answers:

Questions 1 to 5: If you answered true to most of these questions, you're deeply bothered by some aspect of your appearance. Feeling this bad about yourself could interfere with your life. Telling your parents your feelings and visiting your family doctor are your first steps. Research what surgery would involve—cost, hospitalization, recovery time, doctors, etc. Remember, most plastic surgery is not covered by insurance; your doctor can tell you more about this.

Questions 6 to 10: If you answered true to most of these, then you probably have a case of the temporary blues. Teens all experience times when they hate something about themselves, and often that passes as they grow into their bodies. But trying to look like a movie star or muzzling your annoying brother aren't good enough reasons for plastic surgery.

If you answered false, then you're being sensible. You know something is lightweight when you hear it.

cosmetics:
do you get **?**
what you pay for

Does your cosmetics budget blow you out of the water? And are those expensive brands really worth the big bucks? Sure, you want to look gorg, but you don't want to be stupid about it.

Check the answer you think is true.

1
Expensive makeup is the best

- ❑ a) Always.
- ❑ b) Only on sale.
- ❑ c) Low-price brands can be just as good.

2
Makeup artists use only high-priced cosmetics.

- ❑ a) Not true—they experiment with a range of prices.
- ❑ b) They can afford to.
- ❑ c) True.

3
Only the really expensive eye shadow, lipstick, and nail polish come in good colors.

- ❑ a) That's why I go to the department stores.
- ❑ b) If it's expensive, it's in.
- ❑ c) Drugstore brands come in cool new colors, too.

4 Cheap nail polish can ruin your nails.

❑ a) Absolutely not. Remover with acetone is the real culprit.

❑ b) And chips faster, too.

❑ c) That's what my buds say.

5 It's good to buy one majorly expensive cosmetic and stick with it.

❑ a) You get what you pay for.

❑ b) It's better to buy less expensive cosmetics to learn with.

❑ c) So what if fashion changes, at least I look good.

6 Expensive shampoos, conditioners, and styling products do the best job.

❑ a) Overusing any conditioners and styling products can weigh hair down.

❑ b) The more the better.

❑ c) I'm paying for expensive ingredients.

7 If I make my own "natural" beauty products, such as rinses and masks, they won't be as good as expensive ones.

❑ a) How could they?

❑ b) I could try them to see if they work.

❑ c) They might smell weird.

8 Expensive perfumes are sexy.

❑ a) On everything I own.

❑ b) If you don't mind paying for packaging.

❑ c) Less costly fragrances are cool and guys love them!

9 Beauty bonus giveaways in department stores are fun and an inexpensive way to try out samples of expensive cosmetics.

- ❑ a) They're fabulous. Next time you're malling with Mom, let her buy the product; you score the goodies in the bonus present.
- ❑ b) Why bother if I don't like everything in the bonus?
- ❑ c) I don't have time to read the newspapers, so I never know when it's bonus time.

10 My bud told me drugstore-brand cosmetics will make my acne-prone skin break out.

- ❑ a) She's wrong. If they're non-comedogenic, they won't clog your pores.
- ❑ b) Cheap brands are bad for your skin.
- ❑ c) I won't take a chance.

Correct Answers

1. c	6. a
2. a	7. b
3. c	8. c
4. a	9. a
5. b	10. a

1 to 3 correct answers: Beauty School Dropout! It's time for you to get hip to makeup—the most expensive is not always best. Not even close! The pros experiment, so should you.

4 to 7 correct answers: A Beautiful Baby, But. Now it's time to grow up all the way. Learn to be a smart consumer and spend your money with your head too.

8 to 10 correct answers: Beauty Plus Brains! You won't be exploited by expensive packaging and status symbols. You're much too savvy to get caught in an advertising trap, and you make informed decisions.

Beauty Bonus

Want to make your own eye makeup? Mix different colors of shadow into a base of face powder to create your own shades.

What's the
HAPPY MEDIUM
in Makeup?

Nobody likes to look at a cake face, but the right cosmetics can bring out the best in your features. Beauty experts advise us to think about our whole appearance when dressing. In other words, don't go hog-wild making up your face only to forget about your hair. To learn if you're in balance, take this quiz. Check the box that most agrees with your makeup philosophy.

	Too Much	Too Little	Just Right
1. Black liner on lips and eyes	❑	❑	❑
2. Heavy eye shadow	❑	❑	❑
3. Long purple nails	❑	❑	❑
4. Pink shimmery nail polish	❑	❑	❑
5. Soft blusher	❑	❑	❑
6. Light eye shadow	❑	❑	❑
7. Super-fake orange tan	❑	❑	❑
8. A warm glow	❑	❑	❑
9. Raccoon eyes	❑	❑	❑
10. Worn-off lipstick	❑	❑	❑
11. French manicure	❑	❑	❑
12. Bitten-off nails	❑	❑	❑
13. Lip gloss with SPF	❑	❑	❑

	Too Much	Too Little	Just Right
14. Overtweezed eyebrows	❏	❏	❏
15. Clumpy mascara	❏	❏	❏
16. Bushy eyebrows	❏	❏	❏
17. Shaved eyebrows	❏	❏	❏
18. Clear gloss pedicure	❏	❏	❏
19. Black toenail polish	❏	❏	❏
20. Pearly whites	❏	❏	❏
21. Unshaved legs and underarms	❏	❏	❏
22. Uncombed hair	❏	❏	❏
23. Dark roots	❏	❏	❏
24. Swinging hair	❏	❏	❏
25. Natural-looking eyebrows	❏	❏	❏

ANSWERS

1. Too much
2. Too much
3. Too much
4. Just right
5. Just right
6. Just right
7. Too much
8. Just right
9. Too much
10. Too little
11. Just right
12. Too much
13. Just right
14. Too much
15. Too much
16. Too much
17. Too little
18. Just right
19. Too much
20. Just right
21. Too little
22. Too little
23. Too little
24. Just right
25. Just right

Annalee Levine attends John Jay High School in Katonah, New York, where she met her friend Jana Johnson, who is now a junior at the Hotch-kiss School in Lakeville, Connecticut.